Power, Dissent and Democracy
Civil Society and the
State in Ireland

Edited by
Deiric Ó Broin and
Peadar Kirby

A. & A. Farmar

British Library Cataloguing in Publication Data
A CIP catalogue record for this book is available from the British Library

ISBN-13: 978-1-906353-09-4

First published in 2009
by
A. & A. Farmar Ltd
78 Ranelagh Village, Dublin 6, Ireland
Tel +353-1-496 3625 Email afarmar@iol.ie
Website: www.aafarmar.ie

Index by Helen Litton
Typeset and designed by A. & A. Farmar
Cover designed by A. & A. Farmar
Cover photograph by Derek Speirs
Printed and bound by GraphyCems

Power, Dissent and Democracy:
Civil Society and the State in Ireland

Contents

The contributors

John Baker is a Senior Lecturer in Equality Studies at University College Dublin (UCD). He is co-founder of the UCD Equality Studies Centre (1990) and of the UCD School of Social Justice (2005). He is the author of *Arguing for Equality* (1987) and co-author of *Equality: From Theory to Action* (2004/2009) and of *Affective Equality: Who Cares?* (2009). His main area of research is in theoretical issues in Equality Studies (see www.ucd.ie/esc).

Michael Cronin holds a Personal Chair in the Faculty of Humanities and Social Sciences at Dublin City University. He is author of *Translating Ireland: Translation, Languages and Identity* (Cork, 1996); *Across the Lines: Travel, Language, Translation* (Cork, 2000); *Translation and Globalisation* (London, 2003); *Time Tracks: Scenes from the Irish Everyday* (Dublin 2003); *Irish in the New Century/ An Ghaeilge san Aois Nua* (Dublin, 2005), *Translation and Identity* (London, 2006); *The Barrytown Trilogy* (Cork, 2007); *Translation goes to the Movies* (London, 2008). *Transforming Ireland*, co-edited with Peadar Kirby and Debbie Ging will be published by Manchester University Press in spring 2009. He is a Member of the Royal Irish Academy.

Mark Garavan lectures in sociology at the Galway-Mayo Institute of Technology, Castlebar. He has written widely on the sociology of the environment. His PhD research was an investigation into the patterns of Irish environmental activism. He acted as spokesperson for the Rossport Five in 2005. In the 1980s and 1990s he was a social care worker in Dublin and elsewhere, working primarily with homeless people.

Martin Geoghegan is a lecturer in the Department of Applied Social Studies, National University of Ireland, Cork. Prior to his appointment in 2000 he worked in youth and community work for over a decade. His primary research interests are in civil society, social movements, social partnership and governance. His teaching interests are in social research methods, community development and European social policy. He co-authored *The Politics of Community Development* with Fred Powell (Dublin, 2004).

Brian Harvey is an independent social researcher, based in Dublin, concerned with issues of poverty, equality, social policy, community development, the world of NGOs and European integration. He works for voluntary and community organisations, government agencies, institutes, non-governmental organisations, trusts and foundations in both parts of Ireland, in Britain and in continental Europe.

Peadar Kirby is Professor of International Politics and Public Policy at the Department of Politics and Public Administration, University of Limerick. He has published extensively on international development and globalisation, especially in Ireland and Latin America. He is author of *Vulnerability and Violence: The Impact of Globalisation* (Pluto Press, 2006), *Introduction to Latin America: Twenty-First Century Challenges* (Sage Publications, 2003) and *The Celtic Tiger in Distress: Growth with Inequality* (Palgrave Macmillan, 2002). He holds a PhD from the London School of Economics.

Mary Murphy is a lecturer in the Department of Sociology, National University of Ireland, Maynooth. Primarily working in the field of political sociology, her research interests include globalisation and welfare states, civil society, politics of social policy reform, local governance, gender, social security and welfare to work. Prior to becoming an academic, she was National Social Policy Officer in the Society of St Vincent de Paul (1998–2001) and Assistant General Secretary of the Irish National Organisation of the Unemployed (1991–8) and she represented anti-poverty interests in national policy institutions including NESC, NESF and national policy processes.

Catherine Murray, a Pittsburgh native, came to Dublin to work in community development after working as a tenant organiser of formerly homeless individuals in Chicago. She holds a BA in Political Science from Villanova University and an MA in International Relations from Dublin City University. Most recently, she moved back to the US to coordinate grassroots movements to support Senator Barack Obama's presidential campaign. She currently lives and works in Washington, DC.

Deiric Ó Broin is Director of the regional *think and do tank*, NorDubCo, based in Dublin City University. He is also directly

involved, with Ronnie Munck, in the development and implementation of the university's civic engagement strategy. Previously
he was employed as an economic policy analyst in the private
sector. From 1995 to 1997 he worked in the Office of Labour
Affairs in the Department of Enterprise, Trade and Employment,
and in the Office of the Tánaiste. He is a graduate of the Dublin
Institute of Technology (DIT) and University College Dublin,
where he completed a PhD. He lectures on local and regional
economic development and EU policy in the School of Spatial
Planning in DIT.

Fred Powell is Professor of Social Policy at National University of
Ireland, Cork. His most recent publication is The *Politics of Civil
Society: Neoliberalism or Social Left* (Policy Press, 2007).

Paul Rogers is an Associate Faculty Member in the School of
Community Studies in the National College of Ireland and
a practitioner of community development through his work
as the Community Development Co-ordinator with Finglas
Cabra Partnership. He has held this position since 2002 following a brief period as the Partnership's Community Network
and Communications Officer. A native of Coolock on Dublin's
Northside he left school in the 1980s and worked in the cloth-
ing industry for some years. He returned to education as a
full-time mature student in 1996 to study Communications in
Dublin City University. Following his graduation in 1999 he
briefly worked in the IT sector as an Instructional Designer and
completed an MA in Design in Digital Media with the Dublin
Institute of Technology in 2003. He is an advocate of Asset Based
Community Development (ABCD) and sees this as the first essential step to empowerment, believing that communities must
be participants in real change at a local level before they can tackle
structural inequalities.

CHAPTER I

Introduction

Deiric Ó Broin

This collection of essays is the culmination of a seminar series organised by NorDubCo in Dublin City University (DCU) in late 2007. The seminars were organised and led by Peadar Kirby and Deiric Ó Broin. NorDubCo was established in 1996 by the Ballymun Partnership, Finglas Cabra Partnership, Northside Partnership, DCU, Dublin City Council and Fingal County Council to promote the economic, social and civic development of the North Dublin region. The motive force behind NorDubCo's establishment was the shared belief that local government, local development agencies, the local university, local civil society organisations and local communities working together could make a difference to the region.

At the time, a very specific set of challenges faced North Dublin and NorDubCo was configured to address them. However, the recent period of prolonged economic growth has removed some problems while creating in other areas a completely new set of issues to be addressed by the members of NorDubCo. Throughout this period, NorDubCo has worked to ensure that sustainable economic, social and civic development takes place in the region, and to create a positive vision for its community and working life, a vision that seeks to embrace all of the region's communities. NorDubCo has a number of distinct objectives, in particular the development of a new, more inclusive, policy debate, and the promotion of new thinking to influence the economic, social and civic environment.

To achieve these objectives NorDubCo works with representatives from a wide variety of civil society sectors: the business community, local government, the local development sector, public representatives (both local and national), education establishments (secondary, further and higher), the media, and state and semi-state institutions.

The development of these relationships allows NorDubCo to facilitate a broad range of policy discussions between various stakeholders. Underpinning these efforts is the shared belief that a fundamental challenge facing North Dublin is to overcome barriers to shared decision-making. This requires a climate conducive to negotiated governance, i.e. the involvement of variable networks of communities, civil society actors and other stakeholders in the relevant policy formulation and decision-making processes. Developing this form of governance involves building and sustaining a social and civic environment which facilitates and supports such a process and establishing an inclusive decision-making process that is responsive to both the long-term and immediate needs of communities and the infrastructural and developmental requirements of enterprise in the region.

To this end, NorDubCo devised a Public Dialogue Programme based on an understanding that, while civic involvement is the foundation of a thriving, vibrant civil society, a space for dialogue about issues of public importance is often lacking. It is our earnest hope that NorDubCo's Public Dialogue Programme contributes to filling that gap. An important component of our programme is an annual seminar series on issues of contemporary concern. The series has been running since 2001.The aim is not just to present information but to develop a dialogue between presenter and audience and amongst the audience itself, in order to develop a fuller, and more robust, shared understanding of the various issues under discussion.

It was in this context that Peadar Kirby and Deiric Ó Broin devised the parameters for the chapters in this volume. It has become increasingly obvious to those of us involved in discussions and debate about civil society and local and regional development that the last ten years has witnessed something important in Ireland. Concurrent with the expansion of the economy, civil society in Ireland has changed significantly and in a variety of ways. The book follows two earlier volumes that developed out of similar seminar series in DCU. The first, *In the Shadow of the Tiger: New Approaches to Combating Social Exclusion*, was published in 1998 and highlighted the continuing challenge of social exclusion at a time of economic growth and general prosperity. In particular, it examined the potential offered by the area partnerships to address social exclusion in a coherent and socially-embedded manner. The second volume, *Taming the Tiger: Social Exclusion in a Globalised Ireland*, re-examined some of these themes. Given the very significant changes in the global economy it was not surprising that globalisation was a key theme in the book, in particular, the challenge of achieving local economic, social and civic development in the context of powerful globalising processes.

A feature of this book, and those that preceded it, is our desire to combine academic knowledge with the experience of civil society activists and community development practitioners. Brian Harvey, Catherine Murray and Paul Rogers bring a diverse experience of community development both in Ireland and the United States. Peadar Kirby (also an editor), Mark Garavan,[1] John Baker and Mary Murphy combine scholarship with a distinguished engagement with civil society in a wide variety of settings. Michael Cronin, Fred Powell and Martin Geoghegan are well-regarded academic chroniclers of the recent changes in Irish civil society and bring an insightful understanding of its nuances and the challenges it faces. Clare Farrell presented a fascinating paper on the importance of an understanding of social capital in community development but her work commitments did not permit her to contribute to this book.

A new feature of this book is that it is being published by A. & A. Farmar. This publishing house is known for its support of research on Irish civil society and its previous publications have provided a critical understanding of the dynamics of Irish civil society. The editors were delighted that A. & A. Farmar was willing to provide a 'home' for this book and are very grateful for the support and encouragement of Anna Farmar throughout the process.

Themes

Power, Dissent and Democracy seeks to examine the health of civil society in Ireland today, in particular its ability to dissent from and contest the actions of the state in a robust and active way. This is one of civil society's key roles in a mature liberal democracy. The book is divided into three sections that reflect our aim. The first examines the historical development of civil society in Ireland, the second reviews a number of important theoretical issues facing Irish civil society, the third analyses the relationship between civil society and the Irish state,

---

1 Mark Garavan did not participate in the 2007 seminar series but, having heard his paper at a seminar in the University of Limerick, the editors invited him to contribute to the volume. We believe that his chapter is an excellent addition and situates itself well within the seminar series objectives.

in particular the tendency by the state to seek to co-opt and control civil society actors. The book concludes with a chapter outlining a variety of alternatives for Irish civil society.

The three chapters in Section I address very different issues yet there are recurring issues in each, for example, the sustainability of many civil society organisations. In Chapter 2, Peadar Kirby of the University of Limerick and Deiric Ó Broin from NorDubCo offer an overview of the development of Irish civil society; in particular they contrast the robust and activist civil society in the late 19th and early 20th centuries with the current state of civil society in Ireland. Reflecting the importance of the struggle for national independence, particularly in the agrarian, labour and cultural arenas, the authors examine the extent to which important elements of Irish civil society have become significantly less contestatory and the implications of this. In Chapter 3, Brian Harvey, an independent consultant in the community and voluntary sector, details the variety of ways in which the Irish state has recently sought to contain, curtail and redirect the activities of civil society. He offers a picture of a fearful, overbearing, possibly over-reaching state and details the numerous false starts in establishing an appropriate relationship between the state and civil society in Ireland. In Chapter 4 Mary Murphy, from NUI-Maynooth, examines the potential impacts of globalisation on Irish civil society and the extent to which states have attempted, usually unsuccessfully, to control or co-opt civil society. In particular, she asks whether the rejection of the Lisbon Treaty was partly caused by state policy. By co-opting many civil society organisations, the state, in essence, undermined their ability to act as independent advocates of the treaty. In conjunction with Peadar Kirby, she returns to this contention in Chapter 11.

Section II offers three contributions on theoretical issues from respected academics who are also actively involved in civil society organisations. In Chapter 5, John Baker, Head of the School of Social Justice in University College Dublin, examines the idea of equality and its relationship to community development. In particular, he outlines the differences between the theories of liberal egalitarianism and equality of condition and the implications of these differences for community development. In Chapter 6, Michael Cronin, from the Faculty of Humanities and Social Sciences in DCU, reviews the work of the Taskforce on Active Citizenship and the key elements underpinning its findings. He notes the influence of two 'currents of thought', communitarianism and civic republicanism, and argues that, despite the acknowledgement of these influences by the members of the Taskforce, it is clear that the conceptualisation and practice of active citizenship as promulgated by the Taskforce lacks a theory of politics to accompany the notion of active citizenship. He outlines the consequences of this absence and introduces the alternative notion of 'reactive citizenship' which he contends is a more accurate reflection of the Irish situation.

In Chapter 7, Mark Garavan from the Galway-Mayo Institute of Technology, outlines a number of the obstacles arising in the process of public deliberation and reasoning, using the Corrib gas dispute as an example. As a spokesperson for the Rossport Five between 2005 and 2007, he has witnessed at first hand the challenges facing those trying to make 'new ways of looking at the work' and the mutual incomprehension of the parties to the dispute, many of whom inhabit what are to all intents and purposes parallel realities, with very little, if any, interface. He argues that by seeing public debate as similar to a discussion between two people, we misunderstand the nature of the dialogue between the parties. As a result, he contends, we need to create a new language of politics, 'one that can celebrate and articulate aliveness'.

Section III examines the relationship between the state and civil society from a variety of perspectives. In Chapter 8, Fred Powell and Martin Geoghegan, from National University of Ireland, Cork, consider the relationship between civil society and the Irish state through the prism of community development. They review three distinct community development strategies: local development, social partnership and community action, and the interaction between these various approaches since the early 1980s. They conclude that the inclusion of civil society organisations in the Irish social partnership process has been problematic and has resulted in the marginalisation of the direct participatory involvement in the political process, at both local and national levels.

In Chapter 9, Deiric Ó Broin, Director of NorDubCo, examines the institutionalisation of the social partnership process since its introduction in 1987. He places this process in the context of a corporatist-biased and consensus-oriented political system lacking a party structure in the western European sense. Acknowledging that such systems of public governance are not that unusual, he maintains that many organisations are undermined by their perceived co-option by the state. He concludes that the 2008 post-budget protests signify that, despite the support of the partnership process by many, if not most, significant civil society actors, many citizens remain distant from the process and their recent recognition of the efficacy of street protest could lead to the evolution of a more activist civil society in the near future.

In Chapter 10, Catherine Murray and Paul Rogers, both community development practitioners in North Dublin, examine the current policy climate and challenge its impact on community development. They also report on the importance of certain types of social capital to communities campaigning for change. Using a case study they outline the value of linkages outside the specific community network to other community, social and professional networks, and show how the absence of these links can impede the advocacy process. Arguing for a new way of supporting communities through the development of social, cultural and economic capital, they advocate new forms of community-appropriate, socially-embedded investment, including the transfer of assets from statutory agencies to independent, non-profit, community-based organisations.

In Chapter 11, which concludes the book, Peadar Kirby and Mary Murphy critically assess the nature of the state–civil society relationship as it has evolved and offer perspectives on how it might continue to change in the near future. In particular they chart how the state has used a variety of strategies to curtail the contestatory potential of civil society and outline the consequences of the current state–civil society relationship, the absence of political dynamic, of national reform campaigns, of civil society as a positive voice in the 2008 Lisbon Referendum, of conflict in social partnership and of coherent political debate. Emphasising the negative results of these absences the chapter outlines three strategies required to allow civil society to break free of its current unhealthy and unbalanced relationship with the state. Following these recommendation the authors suggest how civil society might reconstitute and reorganise itself in a new, free space. They argue that civil society organisations are most effective at the juncture between the state and the market and that they help to ensure a more equitable trade-off between efficiency and equality considerations. Given the nature of the Irish state's efforts to control civil society, the authors contend that the state has missed an opportunity to develop a mutually beneficial relationship with civil society, a relationship that would provide a partner in the attempt to navigate the increasingly complex and globalised world we inhabit.

Section 1
Civil society in Ireland:
historical development

CHAPTER 2

Creating a parallel state: the development of Irish civil society in the late 19th and early 20th centuries

Deiric Ó Broin and Peadar Kirby

Introduction

This chapter examines the development of civil society in modern Ireland, in particular its roots in the establishment of a myriad of nationalist-inspired artistic, cultural, language, labour, feminist and sporting groups that blossomed in the late 19th century.[1] The first section considers the parallel between today's Ireland and that of the late 19th and early 20th centuries and why this period has some important lessons for 21st-century Ireland's community sector. We then examine the period preceding the late 19th-century growth in Irish civil society when the foundations were laid for the state–civil society struggles out of which the independent Irish state emerged at the beginning of the 20th century. This is followed by an examination of the period 1870–1923 and the creation of a virtual parallel state by Irish civil society. The chapter concludes with an examination of the role civil society could play in the development of a new, more engaged, relationship between citizens and their state.

A curious symmetry

There is a curious symmetry between the present situation and that of the late 19th century. Now, as in the 1890s, the idea that there is a gap in our democracy is gaining currency. There was then, as there is now, a growing recognition of the need to bring the governors and the gov-

---

1 A period that Patrick Maume (1999) refers to as 'The Long Gestation' in Irish nationalist life.

erned into a closer, more engaged and dialogical relationship (Ward, 1994: 60–72). The solution implemented by the British government was to create representative institutions through the Local Government (Ireland) Act, 1898. The assumption was that those chosen to represent the people would be responsive to their interests, even if they did not share their actual circumstances or characteristics (Paseta, 1999: 64–6; Boyce, 1996: 41). This partial solution failed to quell the nation's desire for a more developed sense of political self-determination which found rich expression through an activist civil society.

While the circumstances of the early 21st century may, at first sight, seem very different, there are certain similarities. Now, as then, a sense of malaise at the quality and direction of Irish society is evident, even if it remains without a coherent voice or vocabulary. People who work with the most vulnerable and marginalised in Irish society feel much anger at the skewed priorities of the Irish state and the failure to invest in public services for those who have benefited little from the boom of the 1990s. Irish society remains deeply divided; its divisions are fuelling an alarming growth in violence, in part linked to a criminal economy that has taken deep root. Just as a century ago, the institutions of Irish democracy and of the Irish state seem ill-equipped to deal with this malaise, to provide a sense of direction for our society, and to begin effectively to heal some of its deep rifts. In the eyes of many, we have a political class that panders to international corporate elites and to the new moneyed dominant class that has grown up during the boom, greatly assisted by tax breaks, subsidies and myriad incentives the Irish state makes available to them. No political force has yet emerged to give voice to the malaise and so it is mostly through the initiatives of civil society organisations that needs are being voiced, power being contested and radical action taken.

Ireland is therefore at a time of transition, away from past structures and formations that were the inheritance of the struggles of a century ago, towards what we do not yet know. Now, as then, it is civil society which offers the greatest hope to be the incubator of a new social project for Irish society, one that holds the prospect of laying the foundations of greater justice, equality and sustainability. These constitute the themes of this book, critiquing the attempts to co-opt and neutralise the potential of civil society and mapping out some of the principal challenges. In examining the state–civil society struggles of a century ago, this chapter offers some practical lessons from history, reminding

Irish civil society of its historical roots and the immense achievements of an earlier era.

Setting the context 1800–69

In order to have a clearer understanding of the nature of state–civil society relationships in 19th-century Ireland, it is necessary to grasp the earlier inter-linked factors that helped shape them:

(a) a long period of Irish Catholic decline;
(b) the creation of the British state (Acts of Union 1707 and 1800);
(c) the consolidation of the 1688 settlement (constitutional monarchy and Protestant state);
(d) inter-communal strife in Ireland.

With regard to the dramatic decline in the political and economic power of Irish Catholics, Barnard notes that

> English policy aimed to eradicate Catholicism from sixteenth and seventeenth century Ireland. However, failure to do so led to a more limited although still ambitious scheme to remove its leaders. Government service was closed to those who would not profess Protestantism. Other openings—in the law, education and even skilled crafts—narrowed and sometimes closed. By the early eighteenth century, the only profession in Ireland open to Catholics was medicine (2004: 125).[2]

This process of decline was paralleled by a consolidation of Anglican power in Ireland and the continued polarisation of inter-communal relations. For example, the arrival of evangelical missionaries in the 1740s, whose '"enthusiasm" even drew the ire of Jonathan Swift' (Whelan, 2005: 5) raised several objections by many Catholics to state-funded proselytising.

With regard to the creation of the new British state, Jackson observes that the 'insistent treatment of Ireland as a British dependency'

---

2 For example, in 1692 Catholics were forbidden to take seats in Parliament, in 1716 Catholic peers could no longer sit in the House of Lords, in 1729 Catholics were explicitly barred from voting in parliamentary elections, in 1733 Catholics were barred from the legal professions, and in 1745 marriages between Catholics and Protestants were outlawed. There was some reform of the franchise in 1793 when Catholics were admitted to the 40 Shilling Freeholders Register for county constituencies. However, the Irish Parliament was a 'borough-dominated assembly' and so this reform had a very limited impact (Jackson, 1999: 11).

was made possible both by the British-controlled executive and the 'peculiarly unrepresentative nature of the Irish Parliament' (1999: 7). What was particularly unusual about Ireland was not that property interests should be over-represented or that there should be a religious dimension to political rights, but 'rather that the two principles should be combined in order to exclude two powerful and wealthy confessional communities from representative politics' (ibid.). For example, of the 150 constituencies represented in the Irish House of Commons, 107 were 'close', i.e. 'under the control of an individual or a small group of patrons' (Jackson, 1999: 7). Arguably, the 1798 Rising, the Act of Union and the concurrent abolition of the Irish parliament marked 'the closing statements in a major phase of the long argument between England, the centre of imperial power, and Ireland, the recalcitrant colony' (McLoughlin, 2005: 7). By 1801 the main parameters of Irish Catholic civil society's relationship with the avowedly Anglican British state were in place but the period between then and 1869 was also one of significant change. In the years immediately following the Act of Union between Great Britain and Ireland, the 'belief gained widespread currency that the native population of Ireland, like that of Wales and Scotland, could be made peaceful, industrious and loyal through scripture-based education designed to wean them from their traditional allegiance to Catholicism, preparing them for integration into the Protestant establishment of Church and State' (Whelan, 2005: xvi). This process was part of a broader movement in which Ireland, Scotland and Wales were subjected to an economic and cultural transformation, through which they were acclimatised to the 'new political and economic realities of the nineteenth century' (ibid.).

Irish Catholics' resistance to this process, often articulated by Rev. John MacHale and Daniel O'Connell, and their demands for Catholic Emancipation, and particularly their opposition to the Anglican attempts to implement this new Reformation at local level, greatly increased the political and sectarian tension of the 1820s.[3] Finlay Holmes, the noted historian of the Presbyterian Church in Ireland, argues that one result was to 'sharpen Catholic hostility to Protestantism' (2000: 103). Despite the efforts of Presbyterian ministers like Hamilton Magee to condemn the 'coarse, vulgar and oftentimes most ignorant abuse of

---

3 A period Whelan (2005) refers to as 'The Second Reformation', 'Protestant Crusade' or 'The Bible War in Ireland'.

popery' the movement contributed to the emergence of a new Irish national consciousness, which 'in alliance with resurgent Catholicism, identified Protestantism with Unionism and Orangeism, and English rule' (Holmes, 2000: 103). Concurrently, the 'defeat' of the Reform Act of 1832 which reduced the influence of aristocratic patrons in borough constituencies had the 'effect of releasing demotic urban Protestantism' throughout Ireland (Hoppen, 1989: 20). Working-class Protestants in Belfast, Dublin, Cork, Bandon and Youghal 'suddenly developed effective militant politics of their own' (ibid.). While prosperous Protestants retained a grasp of status, power and responsibility, many began to increasingly depend on a vested interest made up simply of 'the superiority of Protestantism itself' (Hill, 1980: 64–5). Holmes notes that while the Reform Act of 1832 marked the beginning of the 'gradual advance of democracy in Britain', in Ireland it wedded many Protestants to the Union as it 'gave them the security of knowing that they were part of the majority population of a great Protestant nation whose ethos and culture they shared' (2000: 95). These cleavages were to have a profound impact on the development of civil society in Ireland.

The period leading up to the Catholic Emancipation Act of 1829 also saw the development and articulation of a distinct lay Catholic perspective. The British government deemed a 'number of safeguards necessary as accompaniments to emancipation' (Ó Tuathaigh, 1990: 56). These centred on two main conditions: (1) the British government should have some form of control over the appointment of Catholic bishops and possibly of priests; and (2) the British government should provide some contribution to the payment of priests. The Irish bishops indicated their willingness to accept these conditions. However, there were significant differences of opinion between many Irish Catholics regarding these 'safeguards'. By the 1820s there was 'an increasing volume of opinion which was hostile' to the 'safeguards' as part of the Catholic settlement, particularly among the increasingly politically aware Catholic laity in Ireland. The decision by an assertive Catholic laity to oppose their bishops' willingness to compromise with the British government was a key part of the evolution of civil society in Ireland. While the story of the Catholic Church in Ireland in the first half of the 19th century is one of 'increased efficiency and unrelenting expansion' it is also the story of the development of nuanced and sometimes contested relationships within Catholicism, between bishops and priests, and clerics and laity (Ó Tuathaigh, 1990: 56–7). This was even noted by observant visitors such as Gustave de Beaumont.[4]

If the environment in which Irish civil society developed in the 19th century was shaped by a myriad of interactions between political, demographic, religious, social, economic, linguistic and cultural change, the one aspect which 'most struck contemporaries and has exercised historians was that of population growth, its speed, its causes, and effects' (Hoppen, 1989: 34). For example, although no one could ever have denied that Catholics constituted by far the largest confessional group in Ireland, the statistics produced by the Commissioners of Public Instruction in 1834 were shocking to Protestants. The Commission found that 80.9 per cent of the population was Catholic, 10.7 per cent were members of the Church of Ireland and 8.1 per cent were members of the Presbyterian Church. The figures 'confirmed the most optimistic claims of one side and the most extreme fears of the other' (Hoppen, 1989: 60). Henceforth, no matter how much Protestants stressed their superior wealth, education and position, 'the great numerical fact now at last precisely revealed could not be overlooked' (ibid.). Its reverberations throughout the spheres of political and social activity were profound and 'the sharper edge it gave to the concepts of sectarian majority and minority furnished one of the central realities of modern Irish life' (ibid.).

In addition, the period saw the beginning of a movement to undermine the 'established' status of the Anglican Church of Ireland, in particular the payment of tithes by non-Anglicans (Boyce, 1996: 18–22; Stewart, 2001: 147). Opposition to the payment of tithes had been a feature of 'every outbreak of agrarian disorder from the eighteenth century onwards' (Ó Tuathaigh, 1990: 173) and the opposition was a 'compound of religious and economic objections' (ibid.). In terms of conscience, Catholics, Presbyterians and Quakers found it unacceptable that they should have to contribute to the maintenance of a church to which they did not belong. These conscientious factors

---

4 Paralleling his friend Alexis de Tocqueville's visit to America, Gustave de Beaumont travelled through Ireland in the mid-1830s to observe its people and society. In *Ireland*, he chronicles the history of the Irish and offers up a national portrait on the eve of the Great Famine. Published to acclaim in France, *Ireland* remained in print there until 1914. In a devastating critique of British policy in Ireland, Beaumont questioned why a government with such enlightened institutions tolerated such oppression. He was scathing in his depiction of the ruinous state of Ireland, noting the desperation of the Catholics, the misery of repeated famines, the unfair landlord system, and the faults of the aristocracy.

severely aggravated the basic economic objections on which the op-position to tithes was chiefly based. Tithes were a tax on the produce of the land and if not paid could lead to the seizure of property. By the 1830s grievances against tithes were widespread and intense. The British government reacted by providing soldiers and police to protect tithe assessors and process servers, and to keep order at tithe seizures and auctions. Violent clashes occurred. For example, in the summer of 1831 a nervous magistrate ordered the local yeomanry to shoot at a crowd gathered at a tithe auction in Newtownbarry in County Wexford, and 12 people were killed. Later in the year, there were 17 deaths at a clash in Castlepollard in County Westmeath. In December 1831, 12 policemen and a tithe assessor were killed by locals in Carrickshock in County Kilkenny. While the tithe issue was partially resolved by legis-lative measures in the mid-1830s its very existence remained a divisive issue for years to come.

The tithe conflict also contributed to the engendering of the revo-lution in political consciousness among Irish Catholics and strength-ened the Catholic Church as an institution. As the Commission of Public Instruction published their findings, the institutional life of Catholicism was emerging from the many constraints and penalties imposed by the Penal Laws that had combined 'both an only-partially effective attempt to constrain religious practice and a more heartfelt effort to deprive Catholics of landed and political influence' (Hoppen, 1989: 61). By the 1830s, 26 bishops provided an increasingly active leadership and communications with Rome were 'frequent and brisk' (ibid.). Though caution remained the order of the day as regards rela-tions with the British government, a new confidence and self-assurance were slowly establishing themselves. For example, by the early 1850s large and expensive cathedrals had been built, or were in the process of construction, in Carlow, Dublin, Belfast, Killarney, Ballina, Tuam, Ennis, Longford, Armagh and Kilkenny.

These trends were further consolidated by the passing of the Poor Relief (Ireland) Act in 1838, which led to major administrative reform at local level and prompted Catholic religious orders to provide relief, and the Charitable Bequest Act, 1844 which legitimised bequests to Catholic charities and social action groups. Concurrently the Catholic Church furthered its social action programme with:

(a) the introduction of new religious orders, e.g. the Redemptorists, Passionists and Sisters of Mercy, and lay groups,

e.g. Society of St Vincent de Paul;
(b) the opening of new hospitals, e.g. Mater and St John of God;
(c) the opening of new schools for the emerging Catholic middle
class, e.g. Blackrock and Terenure;
(d) the opening of schools by the Christian Brothers and
Presentation Brothers.[5]

Despite the horrendous human and social cost of the Famine, Irish
Catholics had by the 1860s consolidated their position and halted the
seemingly interminable economic and political decline. By the time
the Irish Church Act received royal assent on 26 July 1869 under
Gladstone's 'masterly guidance' the tenuous outlines of the emerging
Irish civil society could be discerned (Acheson, 2002: 200). These in-
cluded strained inter-communal relationships, a confident Catholic
Church, a demoralised and disestablished Anglican Church, a confi-
dent Catholic middle class, and a contested relationship between the
British state and Irish Catholics.

Creating a parallel state, 1870–1923

The disestablishment of the Church of Ireland in 1869 opened an
important vacuum at the heart of Irish civil society that was quickly
filled by a resurgent Catholic Church. But, unlike the religious establishment that it replaced which was very dependent on its close links
with the colonial state, the strength of the Catholic Church lay rather
in an emerging and ever more confident civil society then making
new spaces for itself. The half century from 1870 saw this civil society
begin to challenge the dominance of the colonial establishment, socially, politically, culturally and even economically, and then begin to
replace it, establishing many of the institutions that were to become
the foundations of the independent Irish state that came into existence in December 1922. The Irish case therefore represents what, by
international standards, is a remarkably rich example of the success of
civil society activism in creating the conditions for the emergence of a
radically different form of state, one much more representative of the
majority of the population. How this happened holds many lessons for
the new situation in which Irish civil society finds itself today, caught

---

5 By the early 1820s nuns and teaching brothers provided 70 schools for the middle
classes, 352 free day schools and 9,352 pay schools (Hoppen, 1989: 62–3).

in the dilemma of whether to accommodate itself to the tight embrace of a state which is ever more clearly serving the interests of corporate capital (particularly foreign capital) while neglecting those of its more vulnerable citizens, or to break loose in order to contest both the actions and the nature of that state. In this section we trace the history of the transformation wrought by Irish civil society in the half century prior to independence before drawing out some lessons for civil society today.

The first spaces to be filled were political as the new Irish middle class, predominantly but not entirely Catholic, became convinced that their interests lay in Home Rule. While O'Connell had championed this cause in the 1830s and 1840s through a politics of mass mobilisation, the new economic conditions of post-Famine Ireland saw the emergence of an institutionalised political movement gaining 60 MPs in the 1874 general election and forming a separate Home Rule party at Westminster under the leadership of Isaac Butt. In the 1880s, this movement grew more militant under the leadership of Charles Stewart Parnell and came to forge closer links with the emerging civil society, including the Catholic clergy, but most significantly with leaders of the agrarian struggle some of whom, like Michael Davitt, were veterans of the Fenians. These tactics helped to establish Home Rule firmly on the agenda of British politics where it was finally achieved after the third Home Rule Bill of 1912.

Meanwhile, the Parnell split had severely weakened the leadership of the Irish Parliamentary Party among the ranks of civil society and opened spaces for new political struggles to emerge. These took various forms in response to the needs of different constituencies but the two decades from the Parnell split to the eve of the First World War saw a broadening of the political activism of sectors of Irish civil society far beyond the constitutional agenda of Home Rule. The Irish Trades Union Congress, based on its British namesake, was founded in 1894, signalling the emergence of a distinct, and at times very militant, workers' movement the importance of which tended to be later elided as the nationalist struggle for independence took centre stage. The second Anglo-Boer War of 1899–1902 provided an important occasion for nationalist mobilisation when leaders as diverse as Arthur Griffith, James Connolly, William Butler Yeats and Maud Gonne came together in the Irish Transvaal Committee in support of the struggle of the Boers against the British, seeing in it a parallel nationalist struggle to that of the Irish. The great majority of Irish men who fought in the war did so on the British side, but two Irish brigades went out to support the Boers. In this political ferment two new political parties were founded, Sinn Féin in 1905 and the Labour Party in 1912. Both were to go on to play key roles in the new state that finally emerged.

While the opening of these new political spaces through civil society activism is a familiar one, a parallel activism in the economic sphere is not sufficiently appreciated. Already in the 1880s, Horace Plunkett was founding co-operatives in rural Ireland, including creameries and credit societies. These were brought together in the Irish Agricultural Organisation Society (IAOS) in 1894 and by 1904 there were 778 societies affiliated to it, indicating its broad impact on rural society. In her analysis of the co-operative movement, Tovey emphasises that its aims went beyond simple economic improvement to embrace wider goals of individual empowerment and the regeneration of rural society. While efforts were made to get the support of the state, both financially and in policy terms, she argues that 'the co-operative movement was nevertheless a movement which wanted to bypass state power, in favour of empowering agrarian social groups within their own local relationships' (Tovey, 2001: 328). She sums up:

> It articulated a distinctively agrarian "project for modernity", based on the vision of a relatively uniform small-scale producer society, organised around independent, productive and efficient family farms, which remained the core ideology of most Irish farmer organisations, inside or outside the co-operative movement, up to the 1960s at least (ibid. 336).

In a predominantly rural society, this entailed nothing less than laying the economic and social foundations for a project of equitable and sustainable development.

In 1906, in a similar attempt to rejuvenate Irish industrial life, the Irish Industrial Development Association (IIDA) was founded, grouping associations in Cork, Belfast, Dublin, Galway and Derry. The IIDA sought to promote Irish manufactured goods through the Irish national trade mark (Déanta in Éirinn) which it registered, by pressuring shopkeepers to stock Irish-made goods, by persuading manufacturers to improve the quality of their products, by the production of trade data and by lobbying for direct shipping links with overseas markets. The IAOS and the IIDA indicate the broad and practical economic concerns of the activist civil society of the period, bypassing the state in a form of what can be called 'self-help' politics.

This ever more intense wave of political and economic activism took place amid a ferment of cultural creativity that was radically changing the ways most Irish people saw themselves. While attention is often devoted to what might be regarded as more elitist dimensions of this activity, such as the Abbey Theatre, it must be remembered that the Gaelic Athletic Association (GAA) was founded as early as 1884 and by 1902 it had adopted the provincial structure it still has today, indicating its swift spread around the country. Strongly linked from the beginning with nationalist politics, the GAA must be regarded as one of the most remarkable and enduring expressions of the civil society activism of the period. By contrast, the Gaelic League, which was founded in 1893 to revive Irish as the vernacular language of the country, initially achieved a broad-based following but became a shadow of its former self in the post-independence period. This decline, however, must not obscure the fact that the League had a profoundly formative influence on many of the leaders of the 1916 Rising and was very successful in making the Irish language a central part of the identity of the independent Irish state when it was founded. Furthermore, the League's promotion of Irish as a compulsory requirement for entry to the National University of Ireland (NUI) following its establishment in 1908 brought it into serious conflict with the Catholic bishops who feared this might act as a disincentive to Catholic students who might choose Trinity College instead of the new university. When in 1909 the bishops sacked Fr Michael O'Hickey, the Professor of Irish in Maynooth, for support-ing the League's view, 100,000 people took to the streets of Dublin in his support. A year later, the Senate of the NUI opted to make Irish compulsory for matriculation from 1913 onwards. As Mathews puts it: 'On the surface this was a debate about education policy; however, at a deeper level this was a dispute about the fundamentals of national identity' (Mathews, 2003: 27).

The founding of the women's organisation, Inghinidhe na hÉireann (IÉ) in 1900 as a nationalist response to the visit of Queen Victoria that year is a reminder that Irish civil society of the time was not entirely male dominated. IÉ was both an educational and a lobbying organisa-tion, producing a newspaper *Bean na hÉireann* and going against both the Catholic Church and the nationalist party when it supported the introduction of school means tests in 1908. It supported women's suf-frage as well as nationalist causes and many of the leading civil society women activists of the period were members. In 1914, it merged with the more overtly political organisation Cumann na mBan.

An important characteristic of the civil society activism of the time was the publication of newspapers. Mention has been made of *Bean na hÉireann* but most of the new movements and organisations had their own newspapers among them *An Claidheamh Soluis* (the Gaelic League, weekly), *Irish Homestead* (Irish Agricultural Organisation Society, weekly), Griffith's *The United Irishman* (which pre-dated the founding of Sinn Féin, weekly), and the *Workers' Republic* (Irish Socialist Republican Party, founded and edited by James Connolly, irregular). Other influential publications included Moran's *The Leader* (giving influential expression to the new ideology of an 'Irish Ireland' but in polemical and narrow terms, weekly), and the *All-Ireland Review* (edited by Standish O'Grady who was described by Lady Gregory as a 'fenian unionist' (Mulhall, 1999: 109)). This testifies to a lively intellectual culture of pluralist public and political debate, in marked contrast to the absence of such a culture in contemporary Ireland where a narrow orthodoxy of consensual ideas dominates the media and public debate.

While there has been a tendency to view these various civil society movements as separate from one another, it is interesting that this is not how they were seen at the time. For example, in his 1904 book *Ireland in the New Century*, Horace Plunkett links the co-operative and the industrial movement with the literary and artistic movements of the day and states that the book's aim is to clarify 'the essential unity of the various progressive movements in Ireland' (quoted in Tovey, 2001: 328). Tovey summarises the central objectives of this multifaceted civil society activism as follows:

> At the close of the 19th century, the failure of demands for even limited political independence created a situation in which other forms of independent development and autonomy became [all] the more important—linguistic and cultural, literary, organisational and administrative, and economic. The co-operative movement, like the Gaelic League and the Sinn Féin movement of Arthur Griffith, saw the political vacuum of the period as an opportunity to create social, cultural and economic structures which would enable Ireland to take some control of its own future development, whether formally under British colonial rule or not (ibid. 328).

This quote also rightly identifies the fact that the shared objective was to develop the capacity of society to take control of its own future. To this extent, it was an essentially empowering social movement, very comparable to those that have captured the imagination in Latin America, Eastern Europe, Africa and Asia in our times. Indeed, some of those active in these movements were unionist in their politics and so were not seeking to replace the colonial state. Yet a consequence of this social activism was that foundations were laid of many institutions that later became central to the new independent Irish state, as Mathews recognises:

> Significantly, by 1908 the major cultural, political, and educational institutions of the 'post-British Irish state'—the Gaelic League, the Abbey Theatre, Sinn Féin, and the National University of Ireland—had all been established, largely due to the efforts of the revivalists and with little help from mainstream politicians. With the development of these national institutions and the emergence of a new wave of nationalist newspapers, an infrastructure was put in place which allowed the 'imagining' of the Irish nation (Mathews, 2003: 10).

If a new Irish state emerged from the civil society activism of the half-century that preceded 1922, it is paradoxical that the advent of independence marked the decline of that activism. Some of it may be due to the disillusion brought by the divisions of the Treaty debate and the subsequent civil war. But it was also due to a belief that the new state would now take up many of the causes previously championed by civil society. With very few exceptions, the civil society organisations active in the new state remained very dependent on the state, both ideologically and materially. It needs to be acknowledged also that the state, particularly after Fianna Fáil emerged as its dominant party from 1932 onwards, developed a very effective ability to nip emerging dissent in the bud and to co-opt civil society organisations into a benign but disempowering embrace. Civil society lost the capacity to act as incubator of new social and political projects as it had done in the period between 1870 and 1920.

A rediscovered role for Irish civil society

What, then, are the lessons of this extensive civil society activism for today? The first is the point made by Mathews at the end of the quote above. This is that, at heart, it was an achievement of imagination, namely the re-imagining of what constituted the Irish nation or, to put it in terms that might be more readily used today, the national community. A century earlier, the term the 'Irish nation' was understood to mean the Protestant nation which, in the late 18th century, had struggled for a measure of legislative independence from Britain. A century later, the term 'Irish nation' had come to mean something entirely different and it referred to a far wider section of the Irish population, mostly but not exclusively Catholic in religion, but predominantly nationalist in politics (whether supporting Home Rule or complete separation from Britain). This fundamental shift resulted by and large from the actions of sectors of Irish civil society, most especially through education. A sense of separateness was developed through an alternative reading of history and through various cultural activities that flowed from that—music, dance, sport and language. In other words, people came to see the community to which they belonged in a new way, fostering a sense of what Benedict Anderson called 'imagined community' (Anderson, 1991). While this is usually understood to refer to cultural and political nationalism, the relevance for our day is wider.

Irish society has, certainly over the past century, been characterised by intense debates about identity: who are we as a people and what constitutes our distinctiveness?[6] A new feature of these debates today refers to what are sometimes called 'the new Irish', namely those who have recently immigrated to live in Ireland. Among these are some who are learning the Irish language and indeed earning a living through the language (as teachers, journalists or academic researchers, for example). In these ways, the notion of Irishness that came to dominance through the civil society struggles a century ago is again being questioned and a reconsideration of who constitutes the national community is necessary. In a less recognised way, however, the exclusionary nature of Ireland's recent economic growth, with its growing gap between rich and poor, is also challenging the sense of belonging to Irish society that was taken for granted for much of the 20th century. One manifestation of this is the growth of violent crime and the clear breakdown of a cohesive sense of community. It is primarily the organisations of the community and voluntary sector which are working with these excluded groups (both the 'new Irish' and the poor Irish, sometimes the same people, sometimes not), seeking to integrate them into existing society, often with meagre resources from the state.

What is again required in this situation is a fundamental re-imag-

---

6 At the time of writing (spring 2008), RTÉ was broadcasting yet another series on this subject, entitled *The Importance of being Irish*.

ining of who constitutes the Irish national community, not in some glib rhetorical way but in a way that changes the policy priorities of public bodies and the spending of the resources generated by the Irish economy. The act of reimagining will not in itself change policies but, just as it was necessary a hundred years ago, so today it is a necessary first step to mounting a serious challenge to the priorities of public policy and to the politics that constitute them. In other words, generating a cultural ferment of debate and representation is a necessary condition for the sort of fundamental political change required in Ireland if the values and priorities of organised sectors of today's civil society (within the institutions of social partnership, for example) are to find expression in state policies and actions. Central to this cultural ferment must be a much more determined contestation of state actions (and the actions of dominant elites of Irish society) just as characterised civil society a hundred years ago.

If one of the lessons of a century ago is the importance of the task of re-imagining the national community, a second is the need to use creatively the spaces that open up. This section began by making reference to the space opened by the disestablishment of the Church of Ireland in 1869; another space was opened by the establishment of the NUI in 1908. Reference has also been made to the political space opened by the creation of a structure of local government in 1899, providing many nationalist politicians with the opportunity to learn administrative and electoral skills. Another space opened by the colonial state that was used by civil society was the establishment of the Congested Districts Board in 1891. According to Harvey (2007) this was staffed by some of the leading Victorian social reformers who, in the face of strong political opposition, invested in rural co-operatives. Committees were established in every parish, community organisers were appointed to lead the organisational development of districts and community-based nursing services were introduced. Paradoxically, one of the first decisions of the independent Irish state was to abolish the Congested Districts Board. Harvey explains why: 'With the exception of Michael Davitt, Irish nationalist members of Parliament had never liked the board, for it by-passed their patronage and the co-operative movement which it promoted angered their wealthier political supporters' (Harvey, 2007: 8). These examples show the creative ability of different actors in civil society to use the opportunities available to challenge the status quo of the day.

In our day some new spaces have also opened up through which civil society has a voice. Since the mid 1990s, social partnership has dominated and structured the relationship between civil society or-ganisations and the state. A decade of social partnership has, however, left many civil society activists frustrated and feeling co-opted into a state-dominated political project that serves very few of the objectives of civil society, except rhetorically. With the end of the Celtic Tiger, a space is opening that offers challenging new opportunities for civil society. For, as economic decline begins to hit and Irish people face once again the difficulties of unemployment and low growth rates, a new sense of realism has entered the national debate, allowing a more critical reassessment of the lost opportunities of the boom and the huge deficits it has left. This provides new terrain where the critical voice of civil society can find a resonance. It is also significant that, at long last, some serious reform of local government is being proposed. In Latin America, it was such reforms in the 1990s that opened space for the new parties of the left to cut their teeth, gain administrative experi-ence, and broaden their base of support. For many, municipal power provided the platform from which to gain power at national level. For the leaders of Irish civil society, who aspire to a more just and equitable society, the direct election of mayors and the greater powers (including tax raising powers) that are being discussed for Irish local government, provide a space through which to address the huge challenges that lie ahead. This offers the possibility that civil society could again become the incubator of a new social and political project for Irish society if it could rediscover the creativity, independence of spirit and ambitious sense of national purpose that characterised it a century ago.

CHAPTER 3

Ireland and civil society: reaching the limits of dissent

Brian Harvey

The year 2008 marked the 40th anniversary of 1968 when, throughout Europe, students, young people, community activists and social movements took to the streets to demand a more democratic world. Several hundred community sector activists came together in Dublin on 30 April 2008—but it wasn't to celebrate 'sixty-eight', a year in which most of them had not even been born. Instead, it was a sober assessment of an Irish civil society project in headlong retreat. How had things come to such a grim pass?

Civil society in the new Ireland

The 18th and 19th centuries saw the establishment of an original voluntary sector in the area of hospitals and care of the poor, generally along denominational lines. Voluntary and community organisations were an important part of the original Irish state-building project (see Acheson et al., 2005). The early 20th century saw a proliferation of animated voluntary and community organisations in the areas of rural development, co-operatives, housing of the poor, women's rights, culture and the Irish language.

However, the early years of the Free State provided a difficult background for the continued development of voluntary and community activity. The social policy of the 1920s was austere. Most voluntary hospitals were, through financial starvation, gradually absorbed into local authority and state provision (O'Ferrall, 2000). The aims of the cultural and language organisations were adopted as state objectives and achieved through departments and agencies devised or adapted for that purpose. One could make the case that, between them, co-option and an austere new social policy suffocated the post-independence civil society project.

New forms of voluntary and community activity arose in the 1930s. Muintir na Tíre emerged as a movement for rural development, very much aligned with the political aspirations of the new governing party, Fianna Fáil, led locally by parish priests in an age of resurgent Catholic social action. In Dublin, the new archbishop, John Charles McQuaid, although theologically conservative, established progressive voluntary organisations and institutions to assist the poor, children and emigrants. As Ireland emerged from its wartime isolation, the stage was set for a revival of the civil society project. Departments of Health and Social Welfare were set up. A new dawn broke in 1949 when the inter-party government published the White Paper *Social Security*, setting the Republic on course for a welfare state and universal health service, modelled on Britain. This would have required, as it did in Britain, the enlisting of voluntary organisations to deliver the appropriate social and health services to accompany the new model.

It proved to be a false dawn, for the government collapsed and the White Paper proposals were never implemented. This failure has had consequences to the present day. In Northern Ireland, where the British welfare state was introduced in 1949, the density of voluntary and community organisations, which started from a common base at partition in 1925, grew to twice that of the Republic. There, too, key milestones in voluntary sector development were reached much sooner.[1] In the Republic, the absence of a welfare state meant, conversely, that there was no imperative to develop the voluntary or community sector, or to elaborate a policy accordingly. The Republic charted a course of social exceptionalism, which continues to the present day, in which Irish social spending flatlined while that of our continental European neighbours rose steadily. The next landmark report, by the Commission on Social Welfare (1986), did not attempt to restore the idea of *Social Security*. Instead, it advocated a course of pragmatic incrementalism, whereby the state would build its welfare provision as circumstances permitted, but set new floors and targets to lift people above poverty.

But that is to get ahead of the story. The failure of *Social Security* did not mean that voluntary and community activities did not develop in the years that followed 1949, for they did. The following decades saw

1 For example, the formation of the social service board, the Community Trust.

the emergence of some important voluntary and community services. The stormy 1960s saw the arrival in Ireland of some of the new social movements then sweeping across Europe and caring-and-campaigning organisations such as the Simon Community and Cherish. The 1970s marked the appearance of a distinct 'community' sector, legitimised through the National Committee on Pilot Schemes to Combat Poverty which established resource centres, systematised community development, and brought an ethos of empowerment and participation with programmatic responses to social questions. The 1980s saw the formation of national federations across a range of sectors (among them disability, housing, unemployment) and the rapid professionalisation of the voluntary sector in its methods and staffing. In the 1990s, the voluntary and community sector began to benefit from the country's economic growth. Government funding for the sector rose from €271.8m in 1993 to €1,058m by 2001, up 289 per cent, a trend which has continued.[2] Government funding displaced personal giving as the main source of income for voluntary and community groups. The Irish National Organisation of the Unemployed (INOU), followed by other voluntary and community organisations, was invited to join in the national social partnership agreements.

At first sight, this might look like an upward trajectory in which government came increasingly to recognise and value civil society. In reality, the manner in which the Irish state defined its relationship with the voluntary and community sector went through many evolutions, changes of course, u-turns, inconsistencies and adjustments.

2002: the great upheaval

The Health Act, 1970 established the National Social Service Council, which set down a model of county- and city-based social service council development both to promote voluntary activity and to support community development. The government quickly narrowed this role and then redefined the Council. The National Committee on Pilot Schemes to Combat Poverty was terminated, the government instead establishing, in 1982, a National Community Development Agency, a decision reversed in turn by the subsequent government in 1983.

---

2 Joseph Rowntree Charitable Trust: *Rights and justice work in Ireland* and *Rights and justice work in Ireland—a new base line*, York, 1994 and 2002 respectively. The most recent comprehensive figures available are for 2004, which give a government funding figure of €1,181m (Acheson et al., 2005).

Although commitments to develop a formal policy for voluntary and community activity were first given in 1976, again in 1981 and very visibly in 1990, the policy was not published until 2000 in the form of the White Paper *Supporting Voluntary Activity*. The policy was welcomed by voluntary and community organisations. Not only did the White Paper endorse the policy-making role of voluntary and community organisations, but it also affirmed their right to speak, to independence and to freedom of action. Voluntary activity units were proposed for every government department having a significant relationship with the sector. *Supporting Voluntary Activity* announced an immediate boost to the sector in the form of funding for national networks and federations, and for training and research, to be followed by new systems for multi-annual funding.

Although the parties in the government that had drawn up *Supporting Voluntary Activity* were re-elected in 2002, a totally unexpected policy and organisational upheaval followed. The changes had been nowhere flagged in advance, nor had they been part of the Programme for Government. Although *Supporting Voluntary Activity* formally remained government policy, its key provisions were renounced, the funding scheme was reduced and one strand (research) was scrapped (Harvey, 2003). None of the proposed units were established, ministers breezily telling the Dáil that they had no intention of setting them up. A new department was created, the Department of Community, Rural and Gaeltacht Affairs, which became the principal interlocutor with the sector.

Such an abrupt change merits explanation. Although the long delay in agreeing the policy over 1990–2000 was due to territorial rivalry between government departments, the roots of the problem lay deeper. The changes of course in the 1970s and 1980s around social service councils and action against poverty indicated that the state experienced considerable difficulty in reaching a coherent, consistent view over time as to what should be its relationship with civil society. The change in 2002 may have reflected the unresolved nature of that view. Abrupt shifts in the way the state views this relationship are not unusual, taking place in Northern Ireland in the 1970s, Britain in the 1980s and Slovakia in the 1990s. An analysis of the problems of implementing the White Paper *Supporting Voluntary Activity*, described the voluntary–statutory interface as having become a 'highly contested political space' (Harvey, 2003). The arrival of voluntary and community organisations in social partnership attracted audible negative comment from elected representatives and unspoken but nonetheless real opposition within the public service.

Although this was not expected at the time, the period from 2002 saw a further reconfiguration by the state of that voluntary–statutory relationship. Voluntary, and especially community organisations, were taken aback by its manner and vindictiveness: funding for the Community Workers Co-operative, a critic of government policy, was withdrawn. Support agencies in the Community Development Programme were culled from 13 to 6, with the prospect of their eventual elimination. Funding for national anti-poverty networks ended in 2007, the organisations concerned being transferred to the known insecurities of another scheme. A resource centre (the Carmichael Centre), which once publicly criticised the government, found it almost impossible to obtain funding. Projects in the Community Development Programme were told not to employ policy workers. Under what was called 'the cohesion process', they had to submit their development plans for external endorsement (Bon, 2006).

Such redrawing of contours is not unusual in modern European democracies: indeed the principal chronicler of the period when it took place in Northern Ireland gave one chapter the heading 'The state strikes back'! (McCready, 2000). In their study of how modern non-governmental organisations work with government, European researchers of homelessness noted how rapidly the modern neo-liberal state changes and adapts to new models (Doherty et al., 2005).

Evidence of thinking about a new model may be found in the National Economic and Social Council (NESC) report *The Developmental Welfare State* (NESC, 2005a). Without saying so, this in effect confronted its readers with the unresolved issues arising from the rejection of *Social Security* (1949). Following in the spirit of pragmatic incrementalism of the Commission on Social Welfare Report, it argued for the 'services dividend'. The state should use its new financial largesse to develop social services (such as activation measures) for those who had been most excluded so that our level of public services should at least begin to converge with that of our European neighbours.

The services paradigm

Increasingly, the relationship between the state and civil society came to be defined around services. The health services had begun this process earlier through *Shaping a Healthier Future* (1994), *Enhancing the Partnership* and *Widening the Partnership* (1997) which introduced the principle of service agreements to govern the relationship with voluntary and community organisations. In 2006, when the state began to address child poverty in disadvantaged communities in Tallaght, Ballymun and north Dublin, it set up a new and imaginative arrangement for the development of services through the Prevention and Early Intervention Programme (PEIP), run with voluntary and community groups and jointly funded with a leading philanthropic organisation (Atlantic Philanthropies). In conjunction with philanthropy, the government planned the establishment of a new Centre for Effective Services, designed to promote good practice and professional development.

At first sight, there was much to commend the government's belated interest in the improvement in public services, new institutional arrangements and collaboration with philanthropy. However, some of these developments have been accompanied by a readjustment of the civil society project which poses a problem.

It is at the funding interface that this process of readjustment has been most in evidence. An interesting feature of the service agreements is the way their detailed terms evolved over the years. The original model outlined in *Enhancing the Partnership* envisaged 6 points of obligation on the part of the health boards and 11 on the part of the voluntary agencies. By the time health boards came to put them into effect, the obligations required of the state remained at 6, but the requirements on voluntary agencies had grown exponentially (to 25 in the case of the Western Health Board). Although *Shaping a Healthier Future* declared that service agreements were for large organisations and that they were too formal for smaller organisations for which simplified procedures should be adopted, this was not followed in practice. The standard form was used throughout and the health services seem to have felt uninhibited in extending the full rigour of service agreements to smaller voluntary organisations. Although *Shaping a Healthier Future* promised that voluntary organisations would continue to have a direct input into the overall development of national policy, no such arrangements were put in place.

A second feature of the 'services' paradigm was the convergence of government agendas and those of the philanthropic sector. In Ireland this sector is small, probably worth about €75m a year, and is dominated by one group, Atlantic Philanthropies. Many philanthropic providers are from outside the country. The Joseph Rowntree Charitable Trust was one of a number that challenged government agendas, for it funded what it called a 'rights and justice' programme, building up the capacity of civil society, including many voluntary and community organisations critical of government. However, the PEIP saw, instead, a convergence of the agendas of the government and the philanthropic sector. While this convergence had the merit of enabling new work to be done and a serious issue to be confronted, it was not clear if the implications had been fully thought through. Such a convergence ran the risk that the philanthropic sector would be 'captured' by the state and that any agenda that challenged the state would be isolated and marginalised.[3]

The introduction of the clause §2.8 in the standard Service Level Agreement (SLA) was perhaps the starkest example of the reconfiguration that began in 2002. This reads:

> The [funded] organisation must not use the grant for any of the following: campaigns whose primary purpose is to obtain changes in the law or related government policies, or campaigns whose primary purpose is to persuade people to adopt a particular view on a question of law or public policy.

Organisations working in diverse areas—development aid, childcare, Travellers—were told that if they took money from government, which most do, they may not criticise.[4] The SLA actually goes a stage further: not only is criticism impermissible, but voluntary and community organisations may not even try to 'persuade' people. The concept that persuasion is dangerous may also be seen in a recent ruling by the Revenue Commissioners that a leading national voluntary organisation[5] should be refused a charity number because charities

> must avoid (a) seeking to influence or remedy those causes of poverty which lie in the social, economic and political structures of countries and communities; (b) bringing pressure to bear on a government to procure a change in policies or administrative practices and (c) seeking to eliminate social, economic, political or other injustice and must operate exclusively for charitable purposes.

---

3 For the concept of 'capture', see Grant, 1989.

4 In 2007, outspoken comments by Trócaire on development issues and by Pavee Point on the situation of Roma people encamped on the M50 roundabout quickly led to comments by ministers that it was time that their funding was 'reviewed'.

5 For fear of reprisal the organisation concerned has asked not to be identified.

Perhaps the most sinister development occurred when the government destroyed the Centre for Public Inquiry, a voluntary organisation set up to investigate corruption. The then Minister for Justice, Equality and Law Reform, Mr Michael McDowell, used Dáil privilege to attack its director, precipitating a crisis in which its duly-panicked funders withdrew. What was much less noticed was the discussion of the incident in the Oireachtas. In the Seanad, members of both government and opposition agreed that corruption should only be the concern of the Oireachtas and institutions established by the Oireachtas: it was wholly inappropriate for civil society to have a role in such a sensitive area. This was an interesting viewpoint, for elsewhere in Europe (notably Italy and the new EU member states), sustained progress was made in the struggle against corruption only when civil society organisations were mobilised.

Conclusions

The Irish civil society project, which in the Irish colony 100 years ago played a leading role in shaping the new Irish state, failed to thrive after independence. As we approach the 100th anniversary of the 1916 Rising, the governmental view of civil society is that it should fit into a new 'services' paradigm. Indeed, if we look at the principal articulation of the model, the developmental welfare state, there is no mention of an advocacy role for civil society or for voluntary and community organisations. The National Economic and Social Council strategy document *People, Productivity and Purpose* even uses the interesting phrase 'non-adversarial partnership' (NESC, 2005b: 231–2).

History may give us some clues as to how this strange turn of events came about. The original civil society project was formed in opposition to the British state, hence the presence therein of so many groups concerned with Irish culture, language, politics and the emancipation of women. The civil society projects that emerged in eastern and central Europe in the 1980s were oppositional to the Communist state— indeed, the restoration of the term 'civil society' to the vernacular can largely be attributed to Václav Havel of Czechoslovakia. There, in the socialist countries, Havel and his colleagues were determined to establish a 'civil society space' free of government, a space free to persuade. Such a space is now denied by §2.8 of the Service Level Agreement, a phrase written by the modern-day Gomulkas of the Irish health service. That the Irish state fears a civil society that might dare to try, in its words, to 'persuade' speaks volumes of its multiple insecurities. Michel Peillon once described the Irish state as 'weak but controlling', a telling phrase (Peillon, 2001). Just as a new vision of civil society was formed in the theatres and bars of Prague in the 1980s, so too may the assembly of 30 April 2008 mark a new starting point in Ireland.

CHAPTER 4

What impact might globalisation have on Irish civil society?

Mary Murphy

This chapter has the ambitious aim of reviewing how globalisation might impact on Irish civil society. It introduces key theories to help civil society actors to theorise about globalisation's impact on their work and suggests further reading. The chapter first explores some key definitions and then outlines a theoretical framework. The macro theory focuses on state strategies to reduce civil society's power to articulate conflict about re-distributional issues (Pierson, 1998). Four examples of such state strategies are briefly examined, and the key issue of the strong directive control of the state over civil society is discussed. The chapter concludes that not all civil society organisations have been effectively captured by the state and that it is in both the state's and civil society's interests to have a more independent and balanced civil society and a more open and varied discourse. Finally, the chapter comments on possibilities for civil society organisations.

Key definitions

As Hay (2004) argues, definitions of globalisation are highly contested. A common and widely used definition is that of Held et al. (1999: 6):

> [Globalisation is a] process which embodies a transformation in the spatial organisation of social relations and transactions, assessed in terms of their extensivity, intensity, velocity and impact, generating transcontinental inter-regional flows of activity, interaction and the exercise of power.

While globalisation encompasses economic, social, political, technological and military changes the focus here is on the key words transformation, social relations, and exercise of power—on how the transformational processes associated with increased economic and political global interdependence impact on social relations and the exercise of power between the state and civil society.

Definitions of civil society and community development are just as contested. They overlap with globalisation in that civil society is also concerned with social relations and the exercise of power. Civil society is understood as the voluntary civic and social organisations and institutions that form the basis of a functioning society. It is distinguished from both the state and from wholly commercial or market-based profit-making institutions; however, in practice, there are overlaps between state, market and civil society actors (Daly, 2007). Civil society commonly embraces a diversity of spaces, actors and institutional forms, with various degrees of formality, autonomy and power. The London School of Economics adopts a working definition of civil society that understands it to be populated by organisations such as registered charities, development non-governmental organisations, community groups, women's organisations, faith-based organisations, professional associations, trade unions, self-help groups, social movements, business associations, coalitions and advocacy groups. At a local level, civil society includes community development processes. Drier (2007) makes sense of the numerous definitions of community development by drawing attention to how power is understood in those definitions. While community development can be understood as action to improve a local area, or as a community owned/based service delivery process, the process of a community organising its own political voice is the focus of this chapter.

What then is the relationship between globalisation and civil society (Yeates, 2002)? How does globalisation impact on the power of civil society to articulate its demands? How does civil society relate to other power actors and what is the nature of the power dynamic within and between state and society? In Polanyian[1] terms we expect Irish civil society to put pressure on the state to respond to the social vulnerability associated with globalisation (Kirby, 2002, 2005). The vulnerability arises from global structural economic and social trans-

1 This paper adopts a Polanyian (2001) view, which understands an interdependent relationship between society and the state. The relationship is often expressed in conflictual terms when society, fearing a loss of social well-being as the economy becomes disembedded from society, puts pressure on the state to re-embed the economy and so protect social well-being.

formation that benefits capitalism at the expense of social well-being. Ireland, as one of the world's most globalised states, is particularly sensitive to globalisation. While the impact is already felt in a net loss of traditional manufacturing jobs, the June 2008 announcement by Hibernian Insurance of the relocation of over 500 skilled jobs to India has widened the area of the economy that is exposed to such vulnerability. The impact of globalisation is mediated by national political institutions so we can discern the effects of the pressures of globalisation in the reactions of the domestic state. Given that we expect civil society groups to articulate the tension that society feels in the context of such globalisation, the key puzzle is why this conflictual role is relatively muted in Irish civil society.

The focus here is on how the state manages its distributional conflict with civil society and whether globalisation is associated with shifts in power and interest formation related to it. Paul Pierson (1994, 2001) and Duane Swank (2002) explore how, in the late 1980s, the US and the UK shaped the development of civil society interests in order to limit conflict about the restructuring or retrenching of the welfare state in the context of globalisation. Pierson outlines how Thatcher, in managing the restructuring of the British welfare state, set out systematically to 'break the main source of opposition', the trade union movement. Likewise he documents how Reagan in the US adopted a strategy of 'de-funding the left', withdrawing funding from civil society organisations likely to resist the dismantling of the US welfare system. This raises the question of what strategies the Irish state adopted in the late 1980s in the context of the need to restructure public expenditure, and what strategies it adopted subsequently. Four examples of Irish state strategies are now briefly examined: co-option into social partnership, reshaping discourse, reshaping the community and voluntary sector civil society organisations and restructuring local governance.

Co-option into social partnership

Unlike Reagan and Thatcher's overt strategy of smashing opposition, the Irish state chose to manage the possible dissent of trade unions from social and economic restructuring through a strategy of co-option. Corporatist structures were renewed in 1987, when government faced into a difficult period of retrenchment, re-establishing social partnership. Trade unions, employers and farmers worked in several overlapping institutional spaces to develop consensus on policy strategies and to negotiate and monitor national wage agreements. This enabled governments to 'adopt reforms with reduced electoral and social risks' (Natali and Rhodes, 1998: 7). In 1994, social partnership was broadened to include the National Economic and Social Forum (NESF) and, in 1996, part of the community and voluntary sector was incorporated into partnership structures (Acheson et al., 2004). The sector's 1994 co-option into national corporate structures is unique to Ireland. While this is often regarded positively as indicating the strength of interest groups in Ireland (Healy, 1998), it has also been analysed as a state strategy to silence ideological debate or the sort of alternative political discourse to be expected from a third sector (Broaderick, 2002; Murphy, 2002a). So, while many credit social partnership as the cause of Ireland's more humane welfare trajectory relative to the UK or the US (McCashin 2004; Kennelly and O'Shea, 1997; Daly and Yeates, 2003), others argue that social partnership can, through co-option, limit protest and smother the potential for more radical change (Allen, 2000; Ó Cinnéide, 1998). This relationship between state and society has been described by Broaderick (2002) as a 'smothering embrace'.

Acheson et al. (2004: 197) argue that the state plays a key role 'in structuring the civic space in which voluntary action occurs' and that the 'interaction of state drivers with cultural and ideological forces' shapes voluntary action and development. The sector's capacity to be an effective driver of change has been curtailed both by state (or Fianna Fáil) strategies to control or limit the development of the sector (McCashin, 2004) and by its own failure to act cohesively (Acheson et al., 2004). In this state-controlled space meaningful distributional debate is limited (Acheson et al., 2004; Montague, 2001). Murphy and Kirby (2008: 6) argue that

> the battle for ideas has been won hands down by those with a vested interest in ensuring the state takes an extreme market-friendly approach to public policy and in seeking to avoid debates about redistributive taxation, adequate social spending and provision, and more active state policies to generate more successful domestic productive sectors.

Social partnership performs the role of 'cognitively locking' (Blyth, 2002) Irish discourse into a particular development model. Connolly (2007) explores how this development model constrains and limits the possibilities of anti-poverty strategies. In Gramscian terms, social partnership plays a powerful legitimation role for the Irish state. Through a form of ideological persuasion, it enables a dominant ideology of neo-liberalism to permeate our lives and discourse. Neo-liberalism is accepted as 'common sense', so that no alternative is seen as possible. In social partnership the state has an effective tool to achieve hegemonic power.

Reshaping discourse

Through social partnership and other processes, the state actively attempts to reshape discourse. One concept that has been particularly dominant is that of social capital. Robert Putnam's (2000) treatise on social capital *Bowling Alone* was claimed by the former Taoiseach, Bertie Ahern, to be his bedtime reading. The term 'social capital' has certainly influenced political discourse about civil society in Ireland (NESF, 2003; Taskforce on Active Citizenship, 2007). Ireland has not been alone in this regard. The international spread of policy discourse about social capital demonstrates how globalisation has intensified the speed and scale of international policy transfer. It also draws attention to the role international institutions such as the Organisation for Economic Co-operation and Development (OECD) (2001) and the World Bank play in spreading such discourse.

At the core of social capital is the thesis that relationships or social connections between individuals and communities matter. Social capital is seen as 'the glue that holds society together' (NESF, 2003). While keenly contested in academic debate (Farrell, 2007), the term has been taken up in policy and political discourse as an optimistic 'motherhood and apple pie' concept that promotes a healthy society where communities are bonded together. However, Farrell urges caution, arguing that social capital discourse has successfully distracted attention from the ways in which income, power and other structural inequalities actually deplete social relations. To be meaningful, social capital policy needs to be situated in the context of economic, cultural and political capital. We must treat with caution the political promotion of a solidaristic concept like social capital in the context of dominant overriding mainstream Celtic Tiger neo-liberal values. Solidarity and individualism are difficult bedfellows, so it may be that the discourse of social capital only serves to soften the political discourse of individualism.

Irish public discourse promoting social capital fails to examine the cause of its decline. NESF (2003) showed that, while the level of Irish social capital is average in EU terms, there is lower social engagement among young adults, the elderly, people living in rural and large urban centres, lower socio-economic groups, women and those with a disability or illness. Most of the groups with low social capital are the same as those with high risks of poverty and are found in areas with poor social or public services (CSO, 2007). Growing income inequality impacts negatively on social capital as material poverty pulls social ties apart. There is also a psycho-social impact on people's capacity for trust and reciprocity (Wilkinson, 1996). While social supports may mitigate poverty, they will not overcome it. In fact, as Farrell (2007) argues, poor areas may be relatively high in bonding-type social capital (helping people cope or get by) but low in linking and bridging capital (limiting capacity to get ahead). Therefore, social capital is not, nor should it be portrayed as, a cheap fix for disadvantage.

Social capital discourse has had a particular impact on community development policy. It positively reinforced the need for policies and programmes that can strengthen social relations in and between communities. It is associated with new forms of community development such as asset-based community development (ABCD)(see Chapter 10). These work towards a more functionalist or pragmatic version of community development which promotes social cohesion within and between what may be unequal communities. This may be at the expense of a more political version of community development centred on mobilisation, advocacy, empowerment and social analysis of unequal power relations. It remains to be seen how strong an influence social capital discourse has had on what Currie (2008) has described as the 'sidelining' or 'erosion of the original vision and potential of the Community Development Programme' so that is now low-key, fragmented and individualised (see also Chapter 3).

Reshaping the community and voluntary sector

However, the Irish state's strategy for managing dissent and opposition is not as simple as co-opting and winning ideological hegemony through social partnership. The state also adopted a parallel strategy of reshaping the non-economic interests in Irish civil society, what is usually referred to as the community and voluntary sector. Harvey (2008) argues that civil society finds itself in ever more restrictive funding arrangements and that these are accompanied by greater political control by the state. He observes how the Irish state has, since

2002, institutionalised these relationships. He argues that the state has, proactively, by way of funding, regulation and institutional reform, attempted to orientate the community and voluntary sector (and hence civil society) towards a particular development model. He describes the shift to a more managerialist culture as having an 'asphyxiating' impact on civil society. Thus is described the full extent of the state's attempt to restructure the sector.

This shift illustrates how the Irish state has attempted to manage domestic political tensions and mitigate societal reaction as it subordinates social policy to the needs of the economy. To manage political conflict about the direction of policy restructuring, the state intervened in the community sector. Hay (2004) and Cerny (2002) highlight the important role of globalisation as an ideational process transferring concepts, ideas and language. The ideational influence of the US concept of 'social capital' (and the related concept of 'asset-based community development') has played an important role in shifting concepts of civil society from a conflict-based disputation of re-distributional policy to a more consensus-based understanding of civil society as active citizenship and volunteering.

The 2000 White Paper *Supporting Voluntary Activity* enabled shifts in discourse towards service delivery and social capital. The state has also endeavoured to promote a greater service delivery role for the community and voluntary sector. Generally since 1991 the state promoted the social inclusion role of the non-profit private sector with the local area-based partnerships. Since 1994, employment-support functions including the local employment service have been delegated to local non-statutory agencies. A 1999 White Paper promoted regulation of the community and voluntary sector. NESC (2005a) and NESF (2006) signalled a shift to service contracts requiring a new model of governance where the state moves away from the provision of services to become 'a regulator of rights and standards and enabler of local activist networks' (NESC, 2005a: 206–7).

Harvey argues that part of the strategy was a political decision in 2002 to centralise all funding for civil society in a new Department of Community, Rural and Gaeltacht Affairs and to change the rules so that funds previously administered by arm's length agencies were now under direct departmental and ministerial control (this was reflected in the restructuring of the independent agency Area Development Management (ADM) into Pobal whose board is politically appointed). This politicisation of funding is associated with institutional shifts in third-sector funding.[2] For example, the state has promoted an umbrella group called The Wheel which advocates for service delivery and charity models of civic engagement (Acheson et al., 2004: 189). This shift in power has been at the expense of the Community Platform and an alternative policy agenda of social justice.

Restructuring local governance

How might globalisation impact on local civil society organisations? Competition state theory suggests globalisation poses challenges for nation states. Public governance processes need to adapt quickly and devise mechanisms that allow innovative, though manageable, risks to be taken to meet the diverse local policy agendas arising from the impact of globalisation. The state responds to the challenges posed by globalisation by seeking to strengthen its institutional capacity by reaching up and down to draw new actors into a looser governance network, a process referred to as multi-level governance (Hambleton, 2003; Cerny, 2002). Multi-level governance implies that local, regional, national and supranational authorities interact with each other, vertically and horizontally. This is captured by the imagery of states moving 'upward, downward and outward' (Clarke, 2003: 34). The role of the state changes so that both power and functions shift, at these different levels, between administrative units and between statutory, non-profit and commercial agencies. Such innovation in the politics of place means changes in the nature of power and new local institutions and may mean very different processes in urban[3] and rural contexts. Governance here is defined as 'including government but also

---

2 Funding patterns have shown a discernible shift towards service-providing organisations. The allocation of €18m toward national organisations for 2008–10, the successor to the original White Paper funding, included many service organisations traditionally funded by health boards.

3 Hambleton, Savitch and Stewart (2003) and Sassen (2004) explore how such pressures impact locally and on cities and urban environments. Sassen (2001) identifies global cities as those where wealth and employment creation processes are linked to service industries, particularly financial and legal services, and theorises that they face significant challenges as globalisation becomes wider and deeper in scope. The term 'glurbanisation', or new forms of governance in the urban and through the urban (Jessop, 2002), has been coined to describe and define this new paradigm of local governance in the context of the challenges facing larger cities competing in the global market place (Hoffmann-Martinot and Sellers, 2005).

the looser process of influencing and negotiating with a wider range of public, private and not-for-profit actors, to achieve mutual goals' (Hambleton, 2003: 147). Governing now occurs in a wider range of spheres and includes a broader range of actors than previously. The flexible and innovative capacity associated with multi-level governance is seen as enabling the state to address the threats and opportunities arising from globalisation. Such change is referred as 'a new localism'.

There is mixed opinion as to whether this is a welcome development. For some commentators it represents a positive shift and a meaningful transfer of power 'from hierarchical modes of governance' (preoccupied with vertical relationships and the dominance of governmental authority), via market forms (based on competition and contracts), to 'network forms' (built on trust and a sense of common purposes between partner agencies) (Lepine et al., 2007: 8). Others disagree with this assessment claiming that in nation states, governments retain sufficient power and influence over legal, financial and policy levers to ensure that governance takes place in the 'shadow of hierarchy' (Jessop, 2002: 5). In promoting new forms of governance, is the state empowering others or extending its power over more actors?

Worldwide, various new governance techniques have emerged to enable the planning and delivery of policy. New terms, for example 'glocalisation', have arisen to describe these techniques which include networked local governance, community governance, institutional networking, social co-operation and micro-regulatory networks. These approaches strengthen local government through policy committees and stronger roles for mayors, more active roles for citizens in participative governance, decentralisation or devolution, as well as institutional changes to strengthen local government's capacity for engaging in partnership and networking. Clark (2003: 81) summarises these approaches as a 'new political culture' which also includes a new approach to fiscal management involving service or user charges. These shifts are often facilitated by 'managerialism' where new public management administrative and financial devices—including Service Level Agreements, targets and indicators as well as re-regulation, decentralisation and privatisation—are introduced to maximise local flexibility. There are obvious tensions between the contradictory pulls of participatory governance processes and this type of managerialism (Lister, 2004).

It is possible in the Irish case to associate increased globalisation and state strategies to strengthen local governance. The 1992 and subsequent Irish local development programmes, and the development of various local partnership approaches to manage local sectoral challenges, dominated much of the 1990s. The early 2000s saw a process of Irish local government reform and the 'cohesion process' within the local development sector. As Harvey (2008) argues, since 2002 many local groups, including local area-based partnerships, community development programmes, RAPID teams and local drugs taskforces have been obliged to work within more managerial processes.

Despite these elements of new localism, however, it is questionable whether Ireland has adapted urban governance sufficiently to meet the challenges of globalisation. Urban governance in Ireland is still relatively underdeveloped and there has been no transfer of power or enabling of new actors to play strong governance roles. The tensions relating to the cohesion process, and difficulties associated with RAPID in Dublin city, indicate what happens when values of managerialism clash with community-based local governance process. There are parallel tensions in rural governance. The legal and political clashes between the Minister for Community, Rural and Gaeltacht Affairs, Éamon Ó Cuív and various LEADER organisations during 2008, highlight how the state's attempts to redefine the boundaries of rural governance processes have been met with significant resistance. Attempts at multilevel governance in Ireland are impeded by broader horizontal and vertical dysfunction.[4] There are, for example, acute levels of 'geopolitical atomisation' where individual statutory organisations work in isolation within their own geographical boundaries. Weak local government systems compound the difficulties in rolling out effective metropolitan or rural governance programmes. The 2008 Green Paper on local government reform signals the development of policy in this area including regional governance and the possibility of a directly elected mayor in some local authorities by 2012.

This short journey through Irish local governance reforms shows that the Irish state's attempts to strategise multilevel governance responses to the pressures of globalisation have not necessarily resulted in any transfer of power to civil society actors. Rather, the Irish state has retained and even increased its power over civil society. Local

---

4 These themes are further developed in Murphy and Ó Broin's review of the Dublin RAPID programme (2008) and Murphy's (2007) review of the Dublin cohesion process. Both can be accessed at www.nordubco.ie

groups are living in the 'shadow of hierarchy' (Jessop, 2002: 5). In promoting new forms of governance, the Irish state is restructuring local civil society in its own interests. Some of this renders community and local development work vulnerable to the manipulations of the state. As Craig (cited in Ledwith, 2005: 3) states, the practice of community work tends to be 'drawn into the latest fashions of government policy agendas because that is where the funding practice is dominated by the policy and political context rather than creating it'.

An example illustrating the practical impact of state power over local civil society actors is offered by participants in the NorDubCo seminar that resulted in this book. Local civil society organisations working in the north Dublin area reported how they felt they were prevented from commenting critically on the state's management and treatment of the Roma community camped on the Ballymun M50 roundabout in 2007. This control was often implicit; organisations 'felt' or 'knew' the subtle rules of their relationship with the state required them to be silent about the issues. However, the control was also explicit with officials of more than one statutory agency phoning local civil society actors to remind them that their funding arrangement did not permit them to comment on the situation. One national organisation, Pavee Point, did campaign about the issue of humanitarian treatment of this Roma community. Subsequent threats by the then Minister for Justice, Brian Lenihan, to review Pavee Point's funding illustrate how the state uses funding to control civil society voices.

In summary, then, these examples highlight state–civil society tensions and how, at an ideological, funding and institutional level, the Irish state is managing the distributional and restructuring consequences of global and domestic pressures through the parallel strategies of co-option and control. The state has actively reshaped the ideational and institutional context within which civil society exists. Institutional power, funding and voice shift from a civil society defined by social justice towards a civil society focused on service delivery.

The previous exploration of state strategies to control dissent allowed an examination of how globalisation impacts on the relationship between the state and civil society. Power is at the centre of this examination. The state has, in the context of globalisation, reconfigured the role of civil society organisations away from dissent about redistributive justice and human rights and towards local service delivery in partnership with the state. Roseneil and Williams (2004) are wary of changing relations between the national state, local forms of government, and the institutions, organisations and movements of civil society. They suggest that social actors need to be vigilant about how the state works to re-frame political claims, policy demands and public values. Civil society actors need to constantly ask what are the political, policy and cultural contexts that set the parameters for collective action and public participation. There is a clear need to examine how changing modes of governance and new funding arrangements impact on public participation. They argue that social movements are profoundly shaped by the policy direction of the governments they seek to influence.

The Irish state strategy of co-option and control has already impacted on civil society's capacity to articulate the tensions it feels. It is no surprise that civil society organisations should have found themselves involved in power and institutional and ideational struggles. The competition state theoretical framework exposes the importance of the institutional and political struggle about policy and the emerging tension over the role of civil society and the community and voluntary sector. This space is vital. It is from here that Polanyi's (2001) 'double movement' or societal reaction to commodification is likely to emerge. It is also here that the state will seek to constrain societal power and political energy as it seeks to maintain control and manage political conflict.[5]

While some civil society groups have influenced agenda-setting, delivery issues and income adequacy outcomes much of this discourse has been 'voice without influence' (Lister, 2004). The growing consultative voice of the sector 'has not proved enough to change policy priorities' (Hardiman, 1998: 142). Why is this? The Irish political system advantages groups able to organise and promote their interests (Coleman, 2006). To echo Hardiman (1998: 122):

> We may find that at least part of the explanation for the relative lack of progress in redressing these inequalities may be found in a closer analysis of the patterns of interest representation in the form of party policies and interest group formation.

---

5 Polanyi (2001) anticipated that following a 'movement' towards commodification, society, sensing a diminution of human welfare, will respond in a 'double movement' by pressing the state to protect commodified labour from the excesses of market greed. Society would press the state to decommodify labour. Polanyi clearly differentiates civil society from the state.

Hardiman's (1998) observation that wider civil society and organisations representing the poor are weak and unable to contribute effectively to policy learning, formation and implementation is more potent in 2008 given the fragmentation and territorial division of the community and voluntary sector. This fragmentation limits the sector's capacity to respond to the increased pressures and vulnerabilities of globalisation. In the British context, both Whiteley and Winyard (1987) and Levitas (1988) observed the ease with which governments consciously play groups off against each other and the importance of members of the British anti-poverty sector acting as a single unified lobby. The challenge is to increase the capacity to organise into a more proactive strong vested interest on a longer time scale (Harvey, 2008). If the sector is to respond effectively to the increased pressures and vulnerabilities of globalisation, it has to achieve scale and cohesiveness in Irish civil society. The pluralist power model of many diverse voices informs the development to date of Irish civil society. This should not preclude the possibility of investing in organisational capacity when required to act as a single unified lobby.

How can civil society regain its role in creating a discourse of change and constructing a social crisis out of the serious re-distributional tensions in Ireland? How can it influence local, regional and national discourse? Like other chapters in this volume, this one aims to contribute analysis and to promote awareness. These are essential first steps. However, as Harvey argues, a key strategy has to be to regain some degree of financial independence for civil society organisations. A second key strategy has to be to examine the language of social discourse and reclaim language and concepts from the state. This means reclaiming the debate about active citizenship and articulating it in the language of social justice and political equality rather than social capital. A third important strategy for regaining independence is to review more critically the experience of co-option into social partnership and civil society's practical relationship with the state. Fourthly, as well as the need for organisations to be more critical of the Irish state and its model of social partnership, there is also a need to be more aware of how social partnership processes (both local and national) have had the effect of institutionalising and deskilling civil society organisations from more radical and participative ways of working.

During the 2008 Lisbon Referendum campaign new social movements such as the ecological and anti-military movements organised in alternative ways. Two things are striking about the campaign. An internet analysis of the groups campaigning both for and against the treaty revealed that none of the active campaigning groups had a structured relationship with the state in terms of funding or service delivery contracts. Conversely, no civil society organisation dependant on state funding felt able to participate directly in the campaign. This may have been because of fears about funding. However, it is as likely to be because state control has effectively depoliticised a large section of civil society. While this has obvious implications for the freedom of civil society organisations, the implications for the state are just as serious. Why were there so few civil society organisations articulating a pro-Lisbon Treaty message? For example, it is striking how key pro-Lisbon advocates had to campaign as individuals under the hastily convened Alliance for Europe. In silencing the voice of civil society, the state may be unwittingly silencing the voices of actors who would otherwise be allies in a campaign for a stronger and more social Europe.

The Irish state strategy to co-opt, control and disempower Irish civil society has been largely successful. However, Geoghegan and Powell (2007: 48) argue that there is potential for renewed discourse about alternatives. They write that 'while active citizenship in the community sector may have largely been co-opted as a tool of government, it has the potential to reflexively re-imagine itself as a democratic force where active citizens resist the alienating effect of thin representative democracy—and build counter discourses'.

Ledwith (2005: 7) offers some reassurance here. Recognising that such strategies 'can be uncharted territory and at times frightening and unpredictable' for already vulnerable community groups, she reminds them that there are tools and concepts they can use to make sense of what needs to be done. Importantly, she draws attention to the fact that 'breaking free from a controlling view of the world, one that we are taught to see as inevitable . . . carries the hope that a more socially and environmentally just future based on participatory democracy is a possibility'. The example of conflict and resistance in the 2008 Lisbon Treaty Referendum also indicates that civil society is not fully controlled by the state. A more radical, participative and democratic citizenship is clearly possible. Another and better world is also possible.

Section 11
Civil society in Ireland:
theoretical issues

CHAPTER 5

Liberal equality versus equ
condition: implications for community
development

John Baker

Not so long ago, the idea of equality had fallen out of fashion. Anti-egalitarian forces, particularly in Britain and the United States, were in the ascendancy, boosted by the rise of Thatcherism and the fall of communism. It was never quite so stark in Ireland, where the New Right and neo-liberalism were less triumphalist, but the same currents existed. Yet in the midst of this new political climate, equality was resuscitated, with the passage of the Equality Employment Act 1998, which established the Equality Authority and the Equality Tribunal, the Disability Authority Act 1999, the Equal Status Act 2000 and the Human Rights Commission Act 2000. Equality was also a major element in the Belfast Agreement of 1998 and in the Northern Ireland Act of the same year. These were major achievements arising from years of activism. Had Ireland bucked the international trend and put equality back on the map? Or had something more subtle, or compli-cated, occurred? Had equality come back in an attenuated form, one that served the privileged by eclipsing the radical demands of previous generations?

Such a stark contrast over-simplifies the facts, but it does point to an important distinction between different definitions of equality—or, as I will call them because of their complexity, conceptions of equal-ity. The objective of this chapter is to set out two main conceptions of equality, to highlight some of the differences between them and to suggest why the differences matter for community development. The chapter is based on Baker et al. (2004) to which the reader is referred for a more detailed treatment of the issues.

The main distinction to be made is between *liberal egalitarianism* and *equality of condition*. At the most general level, liberal egalitarianism assumes that there will be major inequalities in the conditions of people's lives, but tries to make those inequalities as fair as possible. By contrast, one can think of equality of condition as trying to reduce, as far as possible, the degree of inequality in the conditions of people's lives. Each is now discussed in more detail.

Liberal egalitarianism

This conception of equality forms the general aspiration of many left-of-centre political movements and might be considered the dominant ideology of the modern welfare state. It is important to note that there are a lot of views that lie to the right of liberal egalitarianism—this is definitely a left-of-centre viewpoint. But it will be suggested later that it does not go far enough.

The two key ideas within liberal egalitarianism are the idea of an *adequate minimum* and the idea of *equality of opportunity*. The first is closely connected to the ideas of basic needs and of poverty. Basically, liberal egalitarians want to ensure that everyone's basic needs are satisfied and that no one is living in poverty. The second idea, equal opportunity, itself has a couple of different interpretations which are returned to below.

What is an adequate minimum? To spell that out in some detail it helps to distinguish between what we call different *dimensions* of equality. The first dimension has to do with what most people think of when the idea of an adequate minimum is mentioned, namely the material *resources* that people need to live a decent life. So, for a start, they will think about an adequate income. If that is combined with the idea of poverty set out in the National Anti-Poverty Strategy, it can be defined as the income necessary for

> having a standard of living which is regarded as acceptable by Irish society generally . . . [and for] participating in activities which are considered the norm for other people in society (Government of Ireland, 1997: 3).

In addition, an adequate minimum of resources should include sufficient access to public services such as water and sanitation, refuse services, health services, schools, and libraries, as well as sufficient savings or wealth to provide a basic level of economic security. It is known that not everyone in Ireland enjoys these basic minimums. The demand by

liberal egalitarians for an adequate minimum of resources is therefore a real and important demand, and one that is recognised across a wide range of public policy objectives even if it is given relatively low priority in budgets and partnership agreements.

Some liberal egalitarians have more ambitious objectives than the relief of poverty. In particular, the liberal egalitarian theorist John Rawls, put forward what he called the 'difference principle', which states that social and economic inequalities are only legitimate if they maximise the standard of living of the worst off (Rawls, 1999). Rawls is often misinterpreted as a defender of 'trickle-down' economics, as if he believed that *any* degree of inequality was acceptable so long as it yielded *some* benefits to the poor. His principle is much more restrictive, stipulating that inequalities are justifiable only if they are necessary for achieving the *highest possible* standard of living for the worst-off group in society. It is very hard to maintain that the degree of inequality we have in Ireland meets this test, since there are many comparable countries where the worst off have a higher standard of living than in Ireland but where there is a lower degree of inequality.

A rather different dimension of equality is what we call *respect and recognition*. What liberal egalitarians tend to identify as an adequate minimum standard in this case are things like the equal public status of all citizens, together with the idea of tolerating differences and allowing people to live as they like within certain 'private' spaces like their families and religions. They accept that there may be important inequalities of esteem among people, but think that everyone should have a certain basic status. It is obvious enough that not everyone living in Ireland has even these basic levels of respect and recognition, not just because many lack the legal status of citizenship—something that has become much more important as a mark of social status than it used to be—but also because being a citizen does not guarantee that your distinctive values and lifestyles are tolerated by other citizens. That is something that Travellers and LGBT (lesbian, gay, bisexual and transgender) people have known for generations. In contemporary Ireland, the two forms of status inequality are interestingly combined in the tendency of some white Irish citizens to perceive everyone with a darker skin as a non-citizen and therefore as inferior. So again, the liberal egalitarian demand for a basic standard of respect and toleration calls for significant reforms in Irish life.

In recent years, the migration into Ireland of people from very different cultures has led to a shift towards what is commonly called multiculturalism. Though it has many varieties, the typical stance of liberal egalitarians towards cultural diversity is to 'live and let live', in effect treating each group's culture as a private space in which they can do as they like, so long as they do not hurt anyone. Seen in this way, multiculturalism is an extension of the ideas of toleration and respect for the private sphere.

A third dimension explained in Baker et al. (2004) is *love, care and solidarity*. Liberal egalitarian theorists do not talk that much about this dimension of equality because they are inclined to see it as a private matter that is not supposed to be dealt with by public policy. To the extent that they do address issues of love, care and solidarity, they tend to define equality negatively in terms of protection from abuse. It would be consistent with the idea of liberal egalitarianism to add a right to minimum standards of care, particularly when thinking about vulnerable people like children and infirm older people. One need hardly labour the point that we have not succeeded in Ireland in achieving these minimum standards, either.

The fourth dimension of equality is *power*. Here the liberal egalitarian idea of an adequate minimum tends to be defined in terms of basic legal and political rights such as freedom of speech, freedom of religion, the right to a fair trial and so on, together with a commitment to liberal democracy, by which is meant the kind of democratic government that is meant to be in place in most western countries. These rights and institutions are meant to protect people against the abuse of power and to give them an adequate basis for influencing the decisions that affect their lives. Most of us in Ireland do enjoy these rights although there are clearly exceptions, and clear shortcomings in the operation of Ireland's liberal-democratic political institutions. Much of the work of recent tribunals has consisted in investigating abuses of power and other ways that democratic processes have fallen short of their professed standards.

The fifth dimension of equality identified is *working and learning*. In relation to work, liberal egalitarians are committed to decent working conditions that are enforced by things like health and safety legislation and other employment laws. With respect to learning, liberal egalitarians are committed to adequate education for citizenship and employment, so that everyone is able to play what is seen as a useful role in society. It seems clear enough that Ireland also fails to meet these standards for significant sections of the population. Working conditions, particularly for migrant workers, are sometimes sub-standard, and Ireland continues to fail to provide an adequate education to all of its children. Liberal egalitarianism therefore poses important challenges to existing practices.

In all of these dimensions liberal egalitarians expect there to be substantial inequalities between people. What they typically say is that these inequalities will be fair if they occur in a context of *equal opportunity*. If everyone has an equal opportunity to do well under each of these headings, then that's the best that anyone interested in the idea of equality can reasonably hope for. What makes things a bit more complicated is that there are also different understandings or conceptions of equal opportunity. In particular, it is important to distinguish between what can be called *formal* equal opportunity or non-discrimination and what Rawls calls *fair* equal opportunity.

Formal equal opportunity can be defined as the idea that in certain situations, and particularly in the case of access to education and access to employment, people's success should depend entirely on their abilities. Formal equal opportunity is generally enforced in western societies, as it is in Ireland, through anti-discrimination legislation which forbids schools and employers from discriminating between applicants on the basis of certain named grounds such as gender, ethnic origin, skin colour and religion. That is the kind of legislation we have in Ireland in the Employment Equality Act and the Equal Status Act. A lot of people would say that formal equal opportunity is a pretty thin ideal, since it doesn't say anything about how people got their skills in the first place. For example, the points system is a perfect example of formal equal opportunity—the Central Applications Office does not allocate university places on the basis of sex or religion or social class. But it strikes many people as unfair that students from middle-class families are much more likely to get into universities than students from working-class families. It is that kind of example that motivates the idea of fair equal opportunity.

Fair equal opportunity is a much stronger idea, insisting that people should not be advantaged or hampered by their social background and that their prospects in life should depend entirely on their own effort and abilities. This does mean that children from working-class backgrounds should have as good a future in life as children from middle-class backgrounds, which of course is not the case at all in Ireland or any other western society (though some of them come a lot closer to the ideal than we do). Quite a lot of lip service is given to this understanding of equal opportunity and it is often assumed that if only we put enough resources into the educational system we could bring it about. That is a very doubtful proposition because as long as there are major inequalities of condition in a society, the privileged are going to find ways of advantaging their children. It is not just that their own educational advantages give their children a head start, but also that they can pay for more books, trips abroad, extra tuition, home computers, internet access and so on. It is perfectly rational for them to do so, particularly in a very unequal society, and the education system on its own cannot stop them. Of course, the structure of the education system will affect the *degree* of inequality of opportunity in a society, and will certainly affect the lives and prospects of working-class students, so that the argument here is not that it does not matter what kind of education system we have. It is simply that one cannot expect the education system to bring about fair equal opportunity on its own.

Equality of condition

As already stated, the idea of liberal egalitarianism is clearly progressive. It certainly aspires to a much fairer society than the one we live in at the moment in Ireland. And as has been pointed out, Irish society has not yet achieved the goals set by liberal egalitarianism. It can be contrasted with the ideal of *equality of condition*. If we go through the different dimensions of equality in the same order, then equality of condition can be set out as follows.

Firstly, under the heading of *resources*, equality of condition calls for much greater equality of income, wealth and access to public services than exists in Ireland at the moment. The ideal is not for completely equal incomes because inequalities of income are justifiable enough if they reflect differences of need or burdens of work. But if those were the only kinds of inequality allowed, it would still mean that, overall, people would have a very similar standard of living. It can be added that the idea of equality of condition recognises that there are other resources that are very unequal in most societies, such as differences in people's social and cultural capital, and that these should be much more equal as well.

Under the heading of *respect and recognition*, equality of condition requires more than the toleration of differences. Quite how to define this higher aspiration is a bit tricky but something that has been found useful is the idea of 'critical interculturalism'. What it is meant to imply is that, although there should certainly be an acceptance of differences among people, there should also be interaction between people with different cultural backgrounds, different religious beliefs, different sexual orientations and so on rather than a simple 'live and let live' attitude, and that there should be space for self- and mutual criticism of people's beliefs. After all, there are very few cultural traditions that are beyond criticism and many of them, including those dominant in Irish society, have been important in reinforcing inequality. So those traditions do need to be open to challenge. Equality of condition also raises doubts about the huge inequalities of esteem that are found in most societies. Can a society that grants some people celebrity status really be a society of equals?

In the dimension of *love, care and solidarity*, equality of condition calls for what might best be described as ample prospects for relations of love, care and solidarity. In other words, we need to accept that these relations are crucially important in most people's lives. Societies should take this into consideration in the way they are organised and the policies they adopt. For example, more attention needs to be paid to so-called 'work-life balance' and therefore to excessive working hours. Proper arrangements should be made for child care, for the care of infirm older people and for the care of other people who need it. We should also attempt to create more caring relationships within workplaces, and we should recognise and facilitate care work.

Turning to *power*, equality of condition retains a commitment to the protection of liberal rights, although it draws a distinction between the basic human right to personal property and the extended property rights that have, in capitalist economies, been at the core of economic inequality. Recognising that group-related inequality can often only be challenged by collective action, it is also sympathetic to some kinds of group rights, such as the right of Travellers or disabled people to represent themselves on relevant decision-making bodies. More generally, equality of condition calls for participatory democracy, by which is meant a form of decision-making that involves widespread participation of ordinary citizens and that extends democracy throughout all the major institutions of society—not just what we currently call politics but other areas like schools, workplaces, families and even religions. Participatory democracy has to be rooted in a democratic social ethos;

and although it is unreasonable to expect everyone to be involved in decision making in every context and at every level, participation at all levels should reflect the social groups affected. We do not have to think of participatory democracy as the opposite of 'representative' democracy, since participatory democracies use representation too. But their representatives should be much more accountable to those they represent. Finally, the participants in a participatory democracy would communicate with each other in a wide range of styles, making it much more possible for all of them to engage in it.

Under the heading of *working and learning*, equality of condition calls for education that contributes to everyone's self-realisation and to satisfying work for all. A very important form of work is that involved in loving and caring, and equality of condition calls for this work to be properly recognised and shared. A society with equality of condition might still have a division of labour, with people specialising in different kinds of work, but it would not be marked by the kinds of inequality we are familiar with, where some people get a lot of satisfaction and personal development from their work while others do work that is nothing but toil. Education would be centred on the self-development of each person, requiring a very different approach to the structure of the curriculum, a very different practice of teaching and a very different, inclusive ethos in educational institutions.

To be systematic, it might well be asked whether there is anything within equality of condition that is similar to the idea of equal opportunity. The answer is that equality of condition accepts the point that people should be free to make what they can of their own lives—it is not up to the state, or society at large, to tell a person what to do with their life. But, in place of the idea of a fair competition for advantage, the type of equal opportunity that is found within equality of condition is the equal enabling and empowering of all. If people are, overall, roughly equal in the conditions of their lives, then that is a way of ensuring that they are equally enabled and empowered to live their own lives.

Returning to the point made about the equality agenda in Irish society at the beginning of this chapter, it can be seen how talk about equality could have become more common in a society that remains severely unequal. The kinds of equality that have become central to Irish discourse and legislation are primarily the weakest forms of liberal egalitarianism—such as anti-discrimination legislation and means-

Table 5.1: Liberal egalitarianism versus equality of condition

Dimensions of equality	Liberal egalitarianism	Equality of condition
Resources	Anti-poverty focus	Substantial equality of resources broadly defined, aimed at satisfying needs and enabling roughly equal standards of living
	Rawls's difference principle (maximise the prospects of the worst off)	
Respect and recognition	Universal Citizenship	Universal Citizenship
	Toleration of differences	'Critical interculturalism': acceptance of diversity; redefined public/private distinction; critical dialogue over cultural differences
	Public/private distinction	Limits to unequal esteem
	Liberal multiculturalism	
Love, care and solidarity	A private matter?	Ample prospects for relations of love, care and solidarity
	Adequate care?	
Power relations	Classic civil and personal rights	Liberal rights but limited property rights; group-related rights
	Liberal democracy	Stronger, more participatory politics
		Extension of democracy to other areas of life
Working and learning	Decent work	Educational and occupational options that give everyone the prospect of self-development and satisfying work
	Basic education; Occupational and educational equal opportunity ('formal' vs 'fair')	

Based on Baker et al. (2004: 43).

tested support for basic needs—as distinct from stronger forms of liberal egalitarianism and radical ideals of equality of condition. Like many other political concepts, there are more and less challenging conceptions of equality, and it is generally the less challenging forms that have become familiar. However, the fact that equality is back on the political agenda provides an opportunity to press for more ambitious goals.

Implications for community development

It should be clear from even this brief overview that there is quite a big difference between liberal egalitarianism and equality of condition, and that equality of condition sets out much more radical objectives for society than liberal egalitarianism (all summarised in Table 5.1). The question to turn to now is 'So what?' In particular, does the difference between liberal egalitarianism and equality of condition matter for community development? All that can be done here is to provide some suggestions as to how the distinction might be important.

The first way it matters concerns the *objectives of community development*. What do we want community development to achieve? Do we just want to ensure that marginalised groups have tolerable lives, but on the whole to aspire to little more? If we also endorse fair equal opportunity, is it simply our aim to ensure that the brightest and best children from these communities rise to positions of privilege? Or should we aim for a society where everyone can look forward to a life roughly as good as anyone else's? What does it say to members of marginalised groups to adopt only a liberal egalitarian set of objectives? These are, of course, rhetorical questions: it is hoped they suggest that the difference does matter. It may not have much effect on day to day issues, where one's aims are often much more limited and sometimes consist in no more than resisting a change for the worse. But how these everyday objectives fit into a wider picture of a good society remains important.

The second way the difference matters is in terms of the process of community development. Should this process be based on inequalities of rights and power, so that although people are consulted on issues of policy, real decision-making lies in the hands of a powerful minority? Or should it be a process of participatory democracy in which everyone has a real say? Should it be a process in which people relate to each other with equal respect and recognition, or one in which there are significant differences of status within community development organisations themselves? Should it be a process in which issues of love and care are left outside the door or one in which relations of love and care are addressed and nurtured? And should community development be a process with a division of labour between interesting and tedious work or one in which everyone can develop themselves through satisfying engagement? Again it is hoped that the questions answer themselves. It is, of course, a struggle to ensure that one's practice conforms to one's ideals, and few succeed entirely in this. But there is a real difference between an organisation that aspires to work as a community of equals and one that does not.

It would be a delusion to believe that equality of condition is on the current political horizon—we would, indeed, live in a better society and a better world if we could even achieve more of the objectives of liberal egalitarianism. But to see liberal egalitarianism as defining society's goals rather than as a stage on the road to a richer vision of society is a truncated vision, and it is therefore important to retain equality of condition as an ideal. And social change can sometimes occur when one least expects it. So rather than ending on a depressing note, it is preferable to quote Arundhati Roy (2003: 75):

> Another world is not only possible, she's on her way. Maybe many of us won't be here to greet her, but on a quiet day, if I listen very carefully, I can hear her breathing.

CHAPTER 6

Active citizenship and its discontents

Michael Cronin

Introduction

On his wanderings around the city of Dublin in June 1904, Leopold Bloom meets his friend Hynes and goes into Davy Byrne's pub for a drink. There they meet up with Alf Bergan and a character who is simply described as the 'citizen'. The citizen in the 'Cyclops' episode is garrulous, opinionated and rarely misses the cue for a rant. After an honours list of the patriot dead that includes the Invincibles, the Young Irelanders, the Fenians and the United Irishmen, he proceeds to hold forth on a 'a new Ireland and new this, that and the other' (Joyce 1977: 303). The citizen invokes a nationalist past as a way of brandishing a nationalist pedigree which he sees as being undermined by the 'foreign', semitic influence of Bloom.

The citizen's cyclopean fixation on ethnic and racial purity at the turn of the 20th century suggests more exclusive than inclusive modes of citizenship. But it is the 'new Ireland' and the 'new this, that and the other' that will make the nameless condition of 'citizen', an explicit and public preoccupation at the turn of the 21st.

Background

In outlining a background to the emergence of the notion of 'active citizenship' in Irish public debate, it is important to identify three core elements, two circumstantial and the third conceptual. The circumstantial elements relate to rapid socio-economic change and the high incidence of migration into the Republic of Ireland over the last 15 years. The conceptual element refers to the two currents of thought, communitarianism and civic republicanism, which provide the ideological framework for the presentation of the concept. High economic growth rates, low unemployment rates and sustained population growth during the years of the economic boom (Keohane and Kühling, 2004: 1) meant that the society experienced considerable changes, changes which were underpinned by a zealous commitment to privatisation, the hegemony of the market and the individualisation of entitlements (Kirby, 2002; Allen, 2007). As the Background Working Paper of the Taskforce on Active Citizenship states, the social consequences were not always positive, '[r]apid economic and social change coupled with changes in expectations and values have also provided a context in which people may be less inclined to know or trust others—whether at the local neighbourhood level or at the level of national politics and governance' (Taskforce on Active Citizenship, 2006: 4). The increase in employment between 1993 and 2004 was in the order of 55 per cent or 650,000. The result was pronounced labour shortages which attracted historically high levels of inward migration to a country traditionally associated with strong, net outward migration. The inflow of immigrants increased from 8,000 per annum in 1996 to 53,000 per annum in 2005. By 2005 over 6 per cent of the population, or 259,000 people, were foreign nationals (Hughes et al. 2007: 218). If Bloom was already beginning to complicate the 'citizen's' narrow view of citizenship then the arrival of many newcomers meant that the fantasy of community based on shared historical experience and tacit values was no longer tenable.

Seeking a way to respond to the two forms of distance, the cooling of inter-personal relationships in instrumentalised market capitalism and the intercultural gap between natives and newcomers, led to an engagement with two bodies of thought, communitarianism, as expressed in the writings of Robert Putnam, and civic republicanism as articulated by Iseult Honohan. The former Taoiseach and leader of Fianna Fáil, Bertie Ahern, expressed his admiration for the work of Putnam, describing him as an 'extraordinary genius' (O'Regan, 2005). Honahan's work is cited in the Background Working Paper, in particular her contribution to *The Report of the Democracy Commission* published by TASC (Honahan, 2005). For Putnam, in his most influential work, *Bowling Alone: The Collapse and Revival of American Community* (2001), the inexorable rise of disconnected individualism is captured in the image of the lone bowler, a stark contrast to the group solidarity of the league teams in a bygone age. Elliott and Lemert summarise Putnam's communitarianism in the following terms:

Civic engagement as opposed to disconnected individualism, cooperative community as opposed to commercialized competition, genuine relationships as opposed to episodic encounters: these are the oppositions through which Putnam summarizes the decline of social life (Elliott and Lemert, 2006: 64).

Three aspects of Honohan's civic republicanism which are picked up by the Taskforce on Active Citizenship are an awareness of inter-dependencies and common economic, social and environmental con-cerns, an attitude of civic self-restraint and an openness to deliberative engagement (Honohan, 2005: 175; Taskforce, 2006: 1–2). In terms of the theoretical influences, both theories are predicated on moving beyond individual predicaments to larger concerns with the social em-beddedness of individuals, even if they accord different weights to the primacy of community, republicans being more sceptical than commu-nitarians of community as an absolute value.

What active citizenship might mean in social practice is hinted at in the Background Working Paper where the UK Home Office is invoked. The Home Office points to three components which would constitute a continuum of active citizenship, namely, civic participation (signing a petition, attending a rally, contacting a political representative), formal volunteering (unpaid help through a group organisation) and informal volunteering (unpaid help for others who are not members of the family) (Home Office Development and Statistics Directorate, 2004: 11). Again, the personal and political are not sundered but placed on a continuous line of social engagement. This engagement is presented as a happy synthesis of liberal and communitarian positions: 'Active citizenship refers to how individuals and communities relate to each other in a pluralist society' (Taskforce on Active Citizenship, 2006: 11). So why is the concept of active citizenship problematic in the Irish context and what do the results of the consultation process reveal about the essential limits to the usefulness of the notion in late modern Ireland?

Power

One word which is conspicuously rare in both the Public Consultation Paper and the Final Report of the Taskforce is 'power.' In essence, what both the articulation of the concept of active citizenship and the struc-turing of the consultation suppose is that all citizens are equal. This is a laudable political principle but a serious misrepresentation of social reality. To claim that the wealthy owner of a stud farm and the junior employee of a government department have the same access to power is a misleading fiction which is instantly negated by the inequities of the fiscal system. The notion that access to socio-economic resources has no bearing on citizens' ability to wield influence and exercise agency is contradicted by the harsh realities of the penal system. Dublin District Court records show that 73.3 per cent of defendants coming before the courts [in 2003–4] were from the most deprived areas of the city and, as Karen Sugrue noted, 'people from the most deprived areas were 49 per cent more likely to be incarcerated than people from the least deprived areas' (Sugrue, 2006: 44). The basic structuring principle of the concept of active citizenship is that power is always horizontal rather than vertical and that all 'stakeholders' are on an equal footing. This conceals what the Canadian sociologist Anthony Wilden has described as the fundamentally 'asymmetrical' nature of power in many societies where power is exercised vertically rather than horizontally. The boss's generous invitation, 'my door is always open', suggests the false symmetry of horizontality whereas in reality the boss's power to hire and fire indicates the vertical nature of the relationship (Wilden, 1980). The false symmetry of relationships implicit in the notion of active citizenship becomes apparent when the outcomes of consultation founder on the embedded power structures of Irish society. The Taskforce Report states that 'there was a clear lack of confidence in some public consultation structures' and observes:

> There is cynicism and a lack of confidence in democratic and some other consultative structures, particularly at local level, with individuals and organisations not feeling that they are genuinely listened to and this is exacerbated by the focus in public services on *customers* rather than *citizens* (Taskforce on Active Citizenship, 2007: 9; emphasis in original).

The Report notes that Ireland has 'very centralised policy-making and service delivery systems' (20) and recognises the need for 'a significant decentralisation of decision-making power and associated reform of revenue-raising capabilities at local level' (25). The most that it can recommend, however, is a greater say for the community and voluntary forums established in each local authority. The whimper is inevitable given that questions of political patronage, clientelism and the running of local party fiefdoms are evacuated from the analysis of the fundamental weakness of local government in Ireland. There is not much hope of understanding how active citizens become passive consumers if the framework of reference is depoliticised, de-historicised and dependant on an analytic grid which fails to explicitly address the reality of the vertical constraints of power in the political life of the Republic.

If a theory of politics is lacking in the conceptualisation and practice of active citizenship as promulgated by the Taskforce, there is not much either in the way of a theory of economics. The absence is in part to do with the strongly liberal notion of political agency which emerges in its report:

> Active Citizenship, by its nature, starts with individuals. While the Government can facilitate, encourage and support it, ultimately Active Citizenship is about how each one of us can play a responsible role wherever we are and whatever our age, status or roles in life (11).

What is striking, apart from the bogus symmetry ('can play a responsible role [...] whatever our age, status or roles in life') is the relentless and repeated emphasis on individual agency which recurs throughout the Taskforce documents. Such an emphasis is not idiosyncratic but is symptomatic of a whole series of state responses to social problems. As Michael Murray noted about the government's 'Race against Waste' campaign 'the individualising of the waste problem, particularly in terms of the degree of attention paid to household waste, has enabled the government to avoid challenging the biggest waste producing sectors by far in Ireland today, namely agriculture, industry, and construction and demolition' (Murray, 2006: 104–5). Climate change has become the latest candidate for the individualisation of responsibility in Ireland with the 'Change Your World. Change the World' mantra. Presenting politico-economic issues as a matter of personal choice and individual preference creates constant pressure to effect a shift from a politicised culture to a privatised culture. 'People increasingly seek personal solutions to social problems in the hope of shutting out the risks, terrors and persecutions that dominate our lives in the global age' (Elliott and Lemert, 2006: 9–10). The paradigm is, of course, not innocent. Over three decades of relentless advocacy of market-based, neo-liberal economic practices at national and European level, with the primacy of the unencumbered trader and the individual consumer, have meant that the default value for government is the individual. Such individualisation of problems has the dual advantage of concealing the real power differentials between different players in society ('you have just as much responsibility as a Tony O'Reilly') and making politics a continuation of market forces where what matters most is consumer preference and the sustainability of Brand Ireland.

What we get are sets of symptoms with no identifiable causes. So, as was noted earlier, the Background Paper speaks vaguely of 'rapid economic and social change' leading to a breakdown of trust but there is no explanation of how we got there. What are the mechanisms for this breakdown? What kind of economic and social change led to this erosion of trust? One obvious place to look is the contemporary economic system which, in the relentless drive to compete, cut costs, and find cheaper and more flexible methods of service delivery, does little to enhance any sense of long-term commitment and loyalty to staff or organisations (Elliott and Lemert, 2006: 91–2; Sennett, 1998). The set of values implicit in the race to the bottom and the instrumentalisation and commodification of human relations cannot but have an effect on the society in which people are workers as well as citizens. If 'obstacles in terms of time' and 'new patterns of work and leisure' (Taskforce on Active Citizenship, 2007: 6) are inhibiting civic participation then an analysis of the structural contribution of contemporary capitalism to the emergence of these obstacles and patterns would seem to be a good place to start. No such analysis is forthcoming, however. Just as the political system is a vague abstraction largely invoked in terms of concerns around electoral participation, so the economy is a nebulous, unexamined backdrop to the lives of the phantasmic citizens. Not only is an analysis of the economy necessary to understand the real conditions for the effective exercise of citizenship but it must also explain why there is a felt need for a debate around citizenship in the first place.

Christian Laval has described the uneasy mixture of omnipotence and vulnerability that characterises citizens and consumers in modern Western economies:

> D'un côté, l'être économique, l'*homo oeconomicus*, est ce pur sujet abstrait des choix quand de l'autre, il est un simple objet utilisable; d'un côté le maître suprême des valeurs, de l'autre une frêle «unité de valeur» dans la grande comptabilité sociale. Cette liberté individuelle, très particulière, celle du choix et de la consommation, est sœur de la sujétion économique (Laval, 2007: 15).[1]

---

1 On the one hand, the economic being, *homo oeconomicus*, is the pure, abstract subject of choices while on the other, he is simply an object to be used; on the one hand the supreme master of value, on the other a fragile 'unit of value' in the great ledger of society. This very specific kind of individual freedom, the freedom to

The coercive rhetoric of self-congratulation, an integral part of boom years discourse in Ireland and which was most assiduously practised by President Mary McAleese, is the child of the 'supreme master'. For the beneficiaries of the boom there was indeed the exhilaration of the rise in disposable income, property values and the freedom to endlessly acquire a succession of consumer goods, most notably, private vehicles (Fahey, 2007: 11–26). But this freedom is shadowed by frailty, by the sense that if value is to be construed in purely utilitarian terms, then one's sense of worth is uniquely determined by economic prospects which by their very nature are subject to change. The scented sirens of 'you're worth it' can soon lead to the shipwreck of 'you're worthless' if the multinational decides to relocate, rationalise, streamline or downsize. Hence the profound unease about the nature of the society the boom brought into being and the political response in terms of the attempts to promote a notion of socially embedded citizenship. By refusing to provide a critical context for the understanding of the operations of the market economy, the Taskforce deals with problems it can neither understand nor resolve. The result is that the active citizen is left to believe in a familiar credo of Faith (in the current politico-economic setup) and Good Works (volunteering).

Global contexts

Markets are now, of course, global and it is a fact regularly noted for comment that Ireland has become one of the most 'globalised' economies and societies in the world. Developments in Irish business, media, sports, education, to name but a few areas, are inconceivable outside the frame of the global. To try to understand what it means to be a citizen in contemporary Ireland of necessity involves a careful examination of how forces outside Ireland are shaping its present and future. Yet, in both the Taskforce's consultation process and the subsequent report, little attention is devoted to what the distinguished Irish sociologist Gerard Delanty has called, 'Citizenship in a global age' (Delanty, 2000). During the consultation process which took place between July and October 2006, there was a plenary meeting of the National Forum on Europe. There is an acknowledgement in the Taskforce Final Report of the dual nature of Irish citizenship, that Irish citizens are both citizens of Ireland and of the European Union. It states

choose and consume, goes hand in hand with economic subjection.

that '[we] need to develop our understanding of the European dimension of Active Citizenship, between and among the people of Europe, within a Europe that is democratic and outward-looking, and which is strengthened and enriched through its cultural diversity' (Taskforce on Active Citizenship, 2007: 2). The vagueness of the aspirations is revealing of the paucity of the analysis.

No evidence is offered of how supra-federal structures like the European Union are impacting in very real ways on the definition and practice of active citizenship in everything from legislation on immigration to the ability of national government to invest in public transport and that of local government to provide free broadband services. In other words, the default value for the notion of active citizenship as it emerges in the Taskforce Report is territorial nationalism. Europe is acknowledged at the beginning of the document but is then almost wholly ignored with the result that there is an air of unreality about conclusions and recommendations that assume that it is business as usual for a nation-state whose macro-political environment has been transformed so dramatically over the last three decades. Europe is not the world, of course, but the world in which Irish citizens also live does not figure in the Taskforce's construction of active citizenship. Ireland's relationship with the United States, for example, not only in terms of the massive inflow of direct investment from there but also of the ubiquitous presence of American cultural products in the Irish mediascape, does not merit a mention and yet among the most powerful drivers of the privatisation of public goods and the individualisation of consumption have been American economic and political interests in Ireland and elsewhere (Allen, 2007). Presenting the global context for Irish citizenship solely (and even then, cursorily) in terms of the European dimension not only excludes important geopolitical and economic partners like the United States but also leads to an even more damaging exclusion which is ironically the globe itself.

In describing the range of activities implied by the notions of engagement and participation, membership of political parties and sporting organisations is mentioned as are voluntary work, caring for a family member or neighbour and 'simply being active and caring about the local neighbourhood, the environment as well as larger global and national issues' (Taskforce on Active Citizenship, 2007: 2). Being active and caring about the 'environment' and 'larger global and national issues' is tacked on almost as an afterthought. A table listing 'trends in active community engagement by organisational type' for the period 2002–6 shows that the percentage of those involved in associations dealing with conservation, environment, ecology, animal rights remained unchanged at a dismal 0.2 per cent (8). This low level of engagement is hardly surprising in view of the fact that the Report itself manages to ignore one of the most fundamental factors that will shape the lives of citizens on this island for the rest of the century and beyond, namely, climate change. The 2007 report of the Intergovernmental Panel on Climate Change (IPCC) argued that a failure to cut greenhouse gas emissions would lead to an average global temperature rise of 4 degrees C and that among the consequences of the rise would be the extinction of hundreds of species, extreme food and water shortages in vulnerable countries and the onset of catastrophic floods which would displace hundreds of millions of people. A survey by the Environmental Protection Agency (EPA) in Ireland showed a surge of 1.9 per cent in greenhouse emissions in 2005, which was the largest annual increase since 2001 (EPA, 2007). As Frank McDonald of *The Irish Times* noted, 'This brings the level of Ireland's emissions to more than 25 per cent above their 1990 levels—nearly double the figure we are required to meet as our contribution to the European Union's commitment under the Kyoto Protocol on Climate Change to cut its overall emissions by 8 per cent' (McDonald, 2007). The EPA figures showed that Ireland's per capita emissions of 11 tonnes per annum were among the highest in the world, exceeded only by the US and Luxembourg. The scale of the imminent ecological catastrophe appears to be scarcely appreciated by the putative architects of active citizenship as carbon taxes are endlessly deferred, energy efficiency standards are only belatedly introduced and motorways and runways and airport terminals are planned to accommodate even more air traffic and urban sprawl.

Census figures for 2006 showed that with 1.96 million cars in Ireland, four out every five households owned at least one car; 57 per cent of all workers drove to work (65 per cent if lorries and vans were included) whereas in 1981, car drivers accounted for less than 39 per cent of commuters. Between 2002 and 2004, the proportion of people walking to work fell from 11.4 per cent to 10.9 per cent, of those cycling to work from 4.4 per cent to 1.9 per cent and of commuters using the bus from 6.7 per cent to 6.1 per cent (Healy, 2007). So, in an era of unprecedented ecological crisis, Ireland's alarming level of car dependency proceeds unchecked and the dangerous degree of reliance on imported fossil fuels is occasionally lamented but every measure from motorway construction to airport development points to the lack of political will for real change. The report of the Taskforce states that '[b]etter public transport remains a key long-term requirement for sustainable communities and Active Citizenship' (2007: 20) yet the unwillingness to engage with the political and economic causes of the global ecological endgame means that there is no meaningful or coherent context for the recommendation. 'Citizenship' is always taken to mean engagement with other human beings but there are virtually no references to the other sentient beings inhabiting the island and how attitudes towards the environment crucially frame the coherence and sustainability of citizenship practices. The difficulty is that although reference is made to 'the vastly changed circumstances of 21st-century Ireland', most of these circumstances from globalisation to climate change are never properly addressed or analysed. The tacit assumption is that the post-Westphalian nation-state, territorially bounded and environmentally invulnerable, is still the dominant frame of reference, almost as if the 'vastly changed circumstances' were a mere figure of speech, not to be taken seriously.

Migration

One change that the Taskforce is forced to acknowledge, however, is migration. As stated earlier, part of the rationale for engaging in the exercise was the changing composition of the Irish population and concerns about what might be a common or a viable basis for citizenship. Seyla Benhabib in a discussion of the notion of citizenship in a liberal democracy argues that citizenship and humanity are indissociable:

> For moderns, the moral equality of individuals qua human beings and their equality as citizens are imbricated in each other. The modern social contract of the nation-state bases its legitimacy on the principle that the consociates of the nation are entitled to equal treatment as rights-bearing persons precisely because they are human beings; citizenship rights rest on this more fundamental moral equality, which individuals enjoy as persons (Benhabib, 2002: 175).

The rights of citizens are based primarily on their human rights, on their rights as members of the human race. As Benhabib observes, however, '"We, the people", is an inherently conflictual formula, containing in its very articulation the constitutive dilemmas of universal respect for human rights and particularistic sovereignty claims' (2002: 177). Implicit in this conflict are the limits to economistic instrumentalism. In other words, liberal democracies cannot look solely to questions of economic well-being within the framework of 'particularistic sovereignty claims' they must also consider a commitment to and a respect for fundamental human rights because to fail to do so is to radically undermine the basis on which citizenship is justified in the first place.

Furthermore, economic developments themselves, whether in the areas of global restructuring, the exponential growth of international financial markets, the continued expansion of tourism worldwide and acute labour shortages, make it 'implausible today to proceed from the counterfactual Rawlsian assumption that "a democratic society can be viewed as a complete and closed social system." A theory of political justice must necessarily include a theory of international justice' (Benhabib, 2002: 168). If the right to exit a society is viewed to be the fundamental right of the citizen of a liberal democracy, as distinct from the restrictions on travel of totalitarian states, then that implies a reciprocal recognition of entry to the society. It is the nature and the consequences of the entry to Irish society which become an overriding preoccupation for the architects of active citizenship. In the recommendations of the Taskforce a whole section is devoted to 'Ethnic and Cultural Diversity and the Challenge of Engaging Newcomers' in which it is argued that 'a balance is required between integration and absorption of norms of civic behaviour here, on the one hand, and, on the other respect for difference in cultures, language and customs' (Taskforce on Active Citizenship, 2007: 22). The recommendations include the establishment of a formal citizenship ceremony and the organisation of courses and the distribution of material on 'Irish history, democratic institutions, culture, language and traditions' (2007: 23). More vaguely, Irish community and voluntary organisations are 'encouraged to undertake proactive initiatives to reach out and engage with newcomers in the society' (2007: 23). The language of 'cultural differences' and 'diversity' would appear to be welcoming and inclusive but if the assumptions are examined there may be less generosity than first appears.

Tim Ingold makes a useful distinction between the 'genealogical model' and the 'relational model' in the representation of human societies. In the genealogical model, essential or important parts of personhood are handed on, fully formed, an endowment from predecessors.

From this perspective, persons enter the life-world, gifted with a set of ready-made attributes from their antecedents. In popular parlance, when people talk about something being in 'the blood' or 'in the genes', the framing reference is the genealogical model. The relational model which has at its heart the notion of pro-generation refers to 'the continual unfolding of an entire field of relationships within which different beings emerge with their particular forms, capacities and dispositions' (Ingold, 2000: 142). Ingold points up the paradoxical consequences of using the genealogical model to think about individuals in the world: 'A genealogy therefore presents a history of persons in the very peculiar form of a history of *relatedness*, which unfolds without regard to people's *relationships*—that is to their experience of involvement, in perception and action, with their human and non-human environments' (2000: 136; emphasis in original). The genealogical model was most explicitly to the fore in the 2004 Citizenship Referendum which very clearly invoked bloodlines and histories of 'relatedness' to racialise definitions of citizenship in Ireland. It goes without saying that the referendum is not mentioned anywhere in the Taskforce documentation on active citizenship. However, there is another dimension to the genealogical model which has implications for how the 'challenge of engaging newcomers' is construed. From a genealogical perspective, difference is rendered primarily as 'diversity', that is to say, individuals are compared to each other by virtue of their essential natures, irrespective of their positioning vis-à-vis one another in the world (Ingold, 2000: 138). What counts here is past histories of relatedness rather than current sets of relationships. Implicit, then, in much of the rhetoric around 'diversity' and 'cultural differences' is a spatialised model of static essences, the multicultural 'tapestry' with its diverse colours, part of the rich inheritance which migrants bring with them. The inherited differences are juxtaposed and the resultant collage is proof positive of the society's cosmopolitan credentials. From a relational perspective, a key dimension to human activity is interaction and change, the emergence of 'forms, capacities and dispositions.' This implies the existence and recognition of reciprocity. It is a key Taskforce recommendation that newcomers seeking Irish citizenship be formally inducted into the society and that '[a]ppropriate information material and education courses could, once developed and established, become a more structured part of the process of becoming an Irish citizen' (Taskforce on Active Citizenship, 2007: 23). However, there is no reciprocal obligation on Irish citizens to familiarise themselves with the history, institutions, culture, language and traditions of newcomers which would recognise that something more is needed than vague aspirations to 'reach out and engage with' migrants and migrant communities. There is a sense that while the multi-ethnic surfaces are to be celebrated, it is genealogical business as usual for the active citizens cordoned off by their transmissible and immutable differences.

The consequences in political and social practice of a genuinely reciprocal understanding of relatedness are nowhere more evident than in the area of language. In an address to the Immigrant Council of Ireland on 4 October 2007 President McAleese argued that the 'single most important, cross-cutting, life-transforming area is language training' and she went on to say: 'If Ireland is to benefit from the extraordinary potential offered by our transformed population, then we need to enable all of our population to realise their full potential and ensure that no one is excluded by a factor as fundamental, as basic as language' (McAleese, 2007). A former Taoiseach, Garret FitzGerald, agreed with the President in an article published in February 2008 in *The Irish Times* entitled, 'It is in our own interests to teach immigrants English' (FitzGerald, 2008). Research conducted as part of the Anti-Racism Plan in 2007 identified language as the 'biggest barrier to integration' (Fitzgerald, 2007) and a report funded by the Clondalkin Partnership and published in 2008 pointed to the 'language barrier' (Mac Cormaic, 2008) as the greatest challenge in the operation of multi-ethnic schools. So, time and again, when language and immigration are raised as issues it is almost exclusively in terms of integration into the dominant language of the host community. As the editorial writer put it in *The Irish Times* of 6 October 2007: 'Use of a common language is the most potent tool in facilitating integration within any society.' So newcomers are repeatedly invited to learn English but there is never any suggestion that the natives might benefit from the extraordinary economic, social and cultural gift of 160 languages being spoken on the island of Ireland over the last two decades (Cronin, 2004).

The strictly unilateral construction of Irish society leads to a formulation of what we might term 'reactive' rather than 'active' citizenship. What is meant by reactive citizenship, in the context of migration, is the construction of citizenship in reaction to external circumstances in a manner that sees citizenship as either a matter of blood rather than soil or defines citizenship wholly in terms of non-reciprocal obligations. The 2004 Citizenship Referendum, the 2008 Immigration, Residence and Protection Bill and the non-reciprocal recommendations on citizenship in the 2007 Taskforce report all speak to a notion of citizenship which is highly reactive and which sees the only duty of civil society as a largely passive respect for 'cultural differences'. As Anthony Elliott and Charles Lemert have noted, multiculturalism is not about holidays for cosmopolitan elites:

> Multiculturalism is, as we say, not about celebrating, even merely 'respecting', social differences. It is about the hard work of living in the real world with both eyes wide open to the seriousness of those differences (Elliott and Lemert, 2006: 151).

Differences both nationally and globally are powerfully mediated by material circumstances, a fact that is carefully concealed by the 'culturalisation' of difference where difference is genealogically constructed as an inherited preference for certain types of food or modes of religious belief. Culture becomes both the new alibi of racism (these people are unacceptable because their culture is not ours) and a euphemistic fog hiding real material differences which affect the life and employment opportunities of migrants.

As the active citizenship process has no engagement with the material dimension to the lives of citizens or those seeking citizenship, it has to practice a language of pious abstraction and studied evasiveness. Nowhere in the documentation, for example, does social class get a mention, yet as we saw earlier in the case of likelihood of incarceration, socio-economic position is highly significant. The Taskforce Report admits that 'concerns exist about the level of inequality in Irish society, and its impact on solidarity between individuals and communities' (Taskforce on Active Citizenship, 2007: 1). In making their recommendations the authors of the report declare that 'it has been necessary, therefore, to keep in mind this wider context of economic development, social equality, accountability and transparency of government' (2007: 15). But the 'wider context' soon fades to nothingness as there is no attribution of agency to account for the 'level of inequality' in Irish society. There is no way of knowing what specific social classes are disproportionately affected by this inequality nor is there any way to identify what might have brought it about in the first place. So, for all the emphasis on pragmatic recommendations, the Active Citizen remains a strangely idealised abstraction, unfettered by any of the pressing material forces which impact so decisively on the lives of men and women in the society.

A noticeable feature of contemporary societies in late modernity is an acute preoccupation with self and by extension with representations that flatter that sense of self importance. In order to escape what Thomas de Zengotita has called the 'universal pain of anonymity' (de Zengotita, 2005: 124), spectators desire ardently to be stars, so that from reality TV to talk radio to Facebook, anybody can, however briefly, play a leading role in the show of the everyday. The relentless exposure to confessional suffering on Irish radio and television is driven, in part, by the intense desire for identification and self-recognition (I, too, know what it is like to suffer and be misunderstood . . .). In a sense, what the notion of active citizenship does is to suggest that the spectators in the political arena can become stars, that they too can play a part in the docudrama of national political life. The notion of active citizenship, then, is highly resonant with the post-Princess Diana mediascape where the floral tributes are centre stage, where the main story becomes not the mourned but the mourners. The self is constantly addressed not only by incessant advertising which appears to single out the individual consumer for special attention but by media representations which make the viewer or the listener feel that the mass media are concerned by their individual uniqueness. As de Zengotita has observed:

> This is a form of flattery so pervasive, so fundamental to the very nature of representation, that it has escaped notice, though it ultimately accounts for the much remarked narcissism of our age. The flattered self is a mediated self, and the alchemy of mediation, the osmotic process through which reality and representation fuse, gets carried into our psyches by the irresistible flattery that goes with being incessantly addressed (2005: 7).

The difficulty with this logic of representational flattery is that the sole criterion for effectiveness is the attention span of the viewer or the purchasing susceptibility of the consumer. In political terms, this translates into the sudden fetishising of themes by the government, whether it be the carefully orchestrated media panic around migrant mothers in Irish maternity hospitals prior to the Citizenship Referendum in 2004 or the mobilisation of the Ryder Cup in 2006 to showcase elite versions of the Irish success story. The theming of politics has all the volatility of market preferences and a characteristic of the themed society is the speed with which issues are brought into the public view only to be abandoned as soon they are perceived to have gone beyond their sell-by date. It is hard not to form the impression that active citizenship has fallen victim to this late modern form of inbuilt obsolescence, a theme that briefly titillated the appetites of politicians and institutional players in the public sphere but whose memory is fading fast in light of the obdurate realities of socio-economic inequality and deeply entrenched relations of power in Irish society. Active citizenship may have got the 'wink of the word' but it is doubtful whether it has ultimately amounted to more than the 'gassing' that powered the jaded monologue of Joyce's bar stool prophet.

CHAPTER 7

Civil society and political argument: how to make sense when no-one is listening

Mark Garavan

Wittgenstein's famous remark in the *Tractatus* (6.522) that 'There are, indeed, things that cannot be put into words. They make themselves manifest' surely has as much application to the cut and thrust of every-day social and political discourse as to the more rarified realm of logic and philosophy. Indeed, if democracy is about anything it is about argument—the contest of competing ideas, views and interests, played out in various formal and informal settings. In fact, it can often seem as if we have nothing but argument. If this is so, then surely everything that needs to be said does indeed get said?

This impression of discursive openness and opportunity seems to apply particularly in the case of civil society actors such as community and residents' groups. For example, in the last few years in Ireland a number of controversies have arisen over environmental issues includ-ing the incinerator proposed for Poolbeg in Dublin, electricity pylons in County Meath, and the Corrib gas pipeline in County Mayo. It seems that many community actors are annoyed about specific issues and are well capable of expressing their disgruntlement.

These actors appear to have little difficulty in articulating their positions, making them known to all who will listen and acting on them by organising protests or through political-legal actions. But is this impression accurate? How do community actors actually fare in these protests? Do they really succeed in expressing their views and arguments? Might they have positions and views that cannot be put into words? Are there aspects—perhaps even crucial aspects—of their campaigns that are not, or cannot be, expressed?

In fact, when some of these civil society or community campaigns are closely examined, it is striking how limited is the scope of contemporary discourse. Rather than engaging in a deep debate on funda-mental issues such as the meaning of 'development', the value of 'com-munity', or the purpose and implications of our economic models, the campaigns are forced onto far narrower ground. Thus, campaigns often appear to be merely NIMBY-style reactions to perceived threats. But are they? Might there be more going on here? Might the campaigns be pointing to a deeper set of concerns? Might it be that the dominant notions of progress and development are being contested at a local, community level?

This last question might seem puzzling, even over-blown, because we don't seem to perceive such a public contest. Definitions and con-cepts of progress and development are rarely heard or articulated in overt terms. This is in part because one economic language-game has prevailed in recent decades—a free-market belief system and model which provides the dominant definitions of concepts such as 'progress' and 'development'. These definitions (or rules of the language-game) are so dominant that even to question them is to risk being labelled as irrational. Marcuse's fear that reality is equated with the rational has come to pass.

Yet politics continues as does community and civil society activism. Issues and concerns must still be talked about in some way—they must be expressed (however inadequately) in words. The challenge is to make sense when there is so much of importance that cannot be said.

Making sense is critical not only for those engaged in national formal politics but also for those who are attempting in more modest ways to achieve specific social, cultural and political change. How can concerns and demands be expressed when the words available are limited by context, convention, rhetoric and relevance? Breaking out of these limits may lead to exposure to charges of irrationality and non-sense and hence, to the likelihood of defeat, or being ignored, in public debate.

I have argued elsewhere that there is frequently much more going on in campaigns, particularly where a local community is mobilised, than may be apparent from the publicly articulated claims of the competing actors (Garavan, 2006b, 2007, 2008). For a start, there are aspects of human experience that cannot be expressed, if for no other reason than that they are visceral and emotive. These visceral and emotive reactions are often central to the positions people take on political and social questions and lie beneath them as motivators and animators of publicly expressed views. Yet they are rarely perceived because, in public debate, there is a discursive structure that suggests or imposes a pattern on what can meaningfully be expressed. Sometimes this structure is largely cultural in character but at other times it is consciously constructed as a means of channelling debate.

This discursive opportunity structure can be defined as the extent to which institutional and political structures permit actors to address what they regard as the causes of conflict, and the extent to which their arguments are recognised as legitimate by their interlocutors and permitted to have an effect on policies and decisions.

Much depends on the openness or closedness of the institutional rules which govern the decision-making (or grievance-resolution) process, particularly the levels of genuine participation permitted to 'informal' interlocutors. The concept of discursive structure implies that discourse is shaped by various rhetorical considerations. In short, actors have their interlocutors in mind when speaking (cf. Edmondson, 2007).

In any event, much that is important—even crucial to our humanity and understanding of our humanity—does not get heard in the formal public sphere. The result is that we do not gain a sense of what is being truly argued about, what is really at stake in apparently discrete and limited campaigns and conflicts. Thus, we rarely have to address fundamental questions and challenges and are not often obliged to consider what is the 'good life' and what it is to be fully human. This is because, in order to be effective and included in 'rational' discussion, campaigns must fashion their presentations in terms that permit them access to a necessary and available audience.

This is why I want to argue that making sense, and thinking we know what is going on in public debate, is not straightforward. Making sense involves social, cultural and political calculations and it takes time. Many issues implicitly raised by, and at stake in, campaigns do not get articulated. Thus public debate often fails to address fundamental issues; they remain largely unexamined in contemporary politics, retaining their status as non-problematic and non-contentious, and do not appear on the political agenda.

It seems therefore that campaigns, civil society actors and social movements are often battling not just entrenched forms of power but also convention, 'normality', 'commonsense', even constructed forms of rationality. They are trying to make new claims, new ways of seeing the world. But this may involve new language, with its attendant assumptions and cultural constructions, and has serious implications for those trying to achieve social and political change. If imagination is limited by what is expressible then we are losing in our public discourse vast realms of what is possible.

In order to illustrate these ideas, we can briefly examine the Corrib gas dispute in County Mayo.[1] It is clear that critical aspects of the conflict between community actors on the one side, and the state and large multinational corporations on the other, are often not heard at all. One rarely articulated element—time—can be taken as an example of the cultural misunderstandings between community and corporate actors which prevent the sides making sense to each other. Time may be difficult to recognise as a conventionally 'political' issue, yet it is critical in this dispute and is perhaps also one of the buried issues of contemporary politics. In looking at battles over 'development' between communities and corporations the concept of time may serve as a useful example of what cannot easily be put into words.

The Corrib gas dispute

The Corrib gas conflict in north Mayo began in the autumn of 2000 and gained particular notoriety in the summer of 2005 when five local men spent 94 days in prison because of their opposition to Shell's proposed gas pipeline in their area. Though this has become a very well-known controversy in Ireland it is arguable that most people would be hard-pressed to describe precisely what it is all 'about'. What is at the heart of the conflict?

Is it about 'safety'? Well, perhaps not, or perhaps not entirely, because although reports by international pipeline experts such as Advantica have concluded that there are no significant safety issues with the proposed pipeline, and the Health and Safety Authority have determined that the refinery poses no significant quantifiable risk, local opposition continues as determined as ever. One can confidently predict that no matter what safety report is produced, it will not stop the local campaign. So might it be about health? Well, here too, the relevant Irish experts—the Environmental Protection Agency—have concluded that the project poses no significant environmental or health risks. Yet

---

1 It should be noted that the author has had a close association with this issue, first for the purposes of sociological research since 2000 and secondly, as a spokesperson for the local campaign from 2005 to early 2007.

the campaign continues. So perhaps the campaign is about trust, or the quality of democracy or community rights? Indeed, as the campaign has progressed, many additional issues have been raised, such as control of natural resources, the perils of globalisation, the wrongdoing of multinational corporations, the loss of national sovereignty. What about the environment? Might it be an environmental campaign?

The Corrib gas campaign is 'about' all of the above but also, in a strange way, about none of them directly. In fact, what this campaign, and probably many others, is 'about' is not easy to discern and identify. This challenges the contemporary understanding of modes of reasoning which implies that actors must be able to articulate their reasons for their positions and to defend them in accordance with a scientifically styled standard of empiricism and rationality.

Campaigns appear to be about particular issues, I suggest, because, in order to make sense, political and social actors must translate their concerns into terms that are relevant to their various interlocutors. They must therefore employ language and concepts in ways that make sense to the other parties. They must consider the cultural and social milieu, the institutional contexts and the political features within which the argument takes place. It is as if these are the discursive contours over which a rational speaker must travel if the desired destination—understanding—is to be reached.

Making sense also involves understanding the conventions that govern meaningful public speech—its procedures, precedents, forms of knowledge, and styles and formats. It means understanding one's interlocutors and trying to discern what would make sense to them. It involves comprehending the wider culture within which debate takes place, particularly that culture's dominant myths, assumptions and worldviews. There are also, of course, various contingent factors at play such as the influence of events and of particular individuals.

If we apply these considerations to the Corrib gas dispute it can be seen how that campaign has been shaped by the requirement to make sense to key interlocutors. Thus, key cultural and socio-political values such as 'progress' and 'development' have not been contested as such, at least in direct and overt terms. The campaign cannot credibly present itself as anti 'progress' or anti 'development'. It may question whether these terms apply in the north Mayo instance but it cannot deny their validity as values and criteria. More importantly, the institutional setting across which the campaign has progressed has indelibly shaped it. At times the campaign is 'about' appropriate land use, at other times 'about' safety or health. This is because the campaign has had to adjust, first, to its various interlocutors and second, to the differing institutional contexts within which the argument is taking place. Table 7.1 sets this out schematically.

Table 7.1: Corrib gas campaign interlocutors and issues

Interlocutor	Issue of relevance
Local authority	Land use
An Bord Pleanála	Land use
Environmental Protection Agency	Pollution control
Health and Safety Authority	Industrial safety
State	Development
Shell	'Consultation' and 'development'
Local public	Health and safety
Wider public	Natural resources
Media	Cyclical attention and novelty
Academics	Social movement theory

Each interlocutor has certain key interests and, to be effective and 'rational', the campaign must address each one within its area of relevance. Thus, at any particular time, the campaign could be about land use, or pollution, or safety. The wider public may be tempted to think that the campaign is about a pipeline because that was the only aspect of the issues they heard about during the Rossport Five's imprisonment in 2005. However, following their release, when it became clear that there were many other issues involved, the public might have lost patience believing that the campaign was moving the goalposts and adding new problems, as indeed was claimed by Shell and the government.

But does naming any particular issue really capture what the campaign is 'about'? For example, contrast the issues named with what Willie Corduff, one of the five men imprisoned in 2005, said when asked directly why he was opposing the project. This was his verbatim response in the more intimate setting of a one-to-one conversation conducted outside the exigencies or demands of the campaign:

> I was born and reared on this farm. It's memories that are making us do what we are doing. My father came here in 1947. The place then was pure bog with a fallen-down house. The memories we have are of the way we were brought

up. Hard times. They're the memories you have and the memories you have to keep. To see someone coming in now and trying to destroy it, as Shell is doing, it kills you. Our footsteps are around the place since we were able to walk. There are memories of our fathers and mothers and how hard they worked to bring us up. This was all bog land. It all had to be reclaimed by hand. Doing corners by spade and shaking a bit of their own seed that the cows had left after them in the shed. It wasn't that they went out and bought seed for they couldn't afford to go out and buy seed. They gathered up the seed that was left after the cow had eaten. They shook it in a corner every year to make it green. That's the reality. It's all memories. You cannot let them die (Garavan, 2006a: 15).

What 'sense' does this make? How does this extraordinary answer fit into any of the categories used by the campaign's various institutional interlocutors? While Corduff's answer is entirely 'rational', employing a mode of reasoning and making perfect sense within his cultural setting, it does not make sense in terms of formal public decision-making. Thus, this articulation—which in some ways captures the emotive-visceral-cultural foundations of the local campaign—has to be translated into terms that can have rhetorical and effective purchase. Nothing said here by Corduff relates to questions of safety or health or pollution. But consider how much is lost as a result.

Corduff is not the only member of the campaign to express what matters to him. Others among the disparate group that comprise the Rossport Five express themselves and their motivations in similar terms.

There was a core group of us who were opposed from the beginning on very good grounds because we had done the research and we were not being fooled. We weren't the usual suspects. We hadn't campaigned against any project in the past. They couldn't label us in that way. We weren't NIMBYs either. We knew the project as planned was wrong and dangerous and we didn't want it anywhere else either. Our opponents tried to make out that we were against development. I don't know of anyone around here, or any other place in Ireland for that matter, who is against development. It depends on what you mean by 'development' (V. McGrath, one of the men imprisoned, in Garavan, 2006a: 176).

My ancestors have lived here in Rossport for many generations, at least six generations, in the same spot along the shore on the northern side of Sruth Fada Conn, that is the estuary of the Glenamoy River that flows into Broadhaven Bay. The home place down by the shore is called Rinn na Rón, where the seals used to congregate and sometimes come ashore. That's where I was born and reared. So we've been here a long time and as you'd expect we have a strong attachment to the land and a deep sense of belonging to the place has been built up over many generations (V. McGrath, ibid.: 157).

If you think back on all we had when we were young. All the freedom we had. I could play anywhere within this whole area on either side of the estuary. That included the Ballanaboy site. We used play in there half the time. And I thought it was grand. It was like fairyland. It will never be again if this project got in. Think of this area gone forever (M. McGrath, wife of one of the imprisoned men, ibid.: 171).

A somewhat more formal expression of the same views was given by another of the imprisoned men.

Real cumulative change is evolutionary: 20 or 30 years is an Asahi-type aberration [the name of a previous industry nearby which had caused much visual and other pollution] . . . My problem with [the company's CEO] and more so with the guardians of our democracy, elected or appointed or just doing a job, is a cultural one of incomprehension. . . . When asked what would be the position of local workers who may have got employment before the proposed terminal ended its tour of duty, [a consultant] answered that by that time they would have enough skills to move on. The whole point of community is not moving on: community is rooted and so builds up strategies and implementations for survival; fish spawn that is free moving has a tiny survival rate. In the round, [he] has made our case—there is no evident interface where these two attitudes can merge . . . [I do not] see any chance of a narrowing of the cultural gap between this civilised community and the flotsam and jetsam that wallow in the wake of the ship of Marathon, Statoil and Enterprise Oil (Ó Seighin submission, An Bord Pleanála Oral Hearing, Ballina, February 2002).

Here is a distinct mode of argument, rooted in a particular set of assumptions about what makes sense and what constitutes, in Edmondson's rich phrase, 'wisdom' (2008). It differs from the mode based on stylised notions of scientific reasoning that is often presented as the only reasonable way to argue. Yet, as Edmondson proposes:

Many people seem to believe that there is an invariant, recognisable activity known as reasoning, and that if everyone can be brought to practice it competently, consensus will be the outcome. The exhortation 'Let's be reasonable about this,' is often used by politicians to imply that reasonableness is a laid-out path such that everyone walking it must arrive sooner or later at the same conclusion (Edmondson, 2008, p. 343).

In reality, not only are there different modes of reasoning at play in many locally-based and civil society campaigns, there is also in practice an argument about what is really meant by key concepts of modernisation such as progress and development. But this is often implicit rather than overt so that observers need to be alert to subtlety and nuance. If they are not expressed or heard, these alternate understandings and different ways of seeing the world lie buried within campaigns.

Attitudes to time

A particular manifestation of the cultural differences between the Corrib gas antagonists was their attitude to time. For example, the developers of the pipeline and the local community operated according to very different conceptions of time and quite distinct time regimes. Among many points of conflict and misunderstanding this was a key driver of discord. In examining the different approaches to time we can see how community actors and civil society movements may be marginalised because their sets of meanings are regarded as less reasonable, even less rational. Thus, multinational corporations operate according to time regimes that are immediate and demarcated in linear time sequences. They have quarterly and annual reports, sequential profit growth targets and detailed timelines for the rolling out of projects. This way of organising time corresponds with dominant notions of time in modernity.

This is not to argue that communities hold to an idealised traditional sense of time in some Weberian manner but rather to point out that media and other commentators are not alert to these differences in ways of thinking about time. They fall outside the conventional rubric of conflicts regarding 'environment' or 'safety'. Time itself appears an incontestable and non-problematic concept even though, as Foucault has demonstrated, the eradication of idleness and the organising of time is a central feature of modernisation.

Three aspects to this cultural interface between the community and Shell on the question of time can be identified. First, how much time each side judged as appropriate to spend on dialogue or consultation. Second, how much time each thought it took to belong to the community. Finally, the timescales judged as appropriate for assessing the benefits which development would bring to the community. In each case the company insisted on short timescales while the community actors preferred much longer periods.

Soundbite presentation v. 'unravelling'

These differences can be explored best through quoting the various actors. The first quotation is the company's assertion of its desire to dialogue with local people no matter how long it might take. This represents an extraordinary claim to discursive openness and collaboration.

> Consultation with relevant stakeholders is an integral part of the business, particularly with regard to operations that may generate local community concerns. The views and interests of such communities are of fundamental importance and are an established part of a project's requirements. They are addressed seriously irrespective of whether they may impact on project schedules. The Corrib Project in Ireland is currently undergoing extensive consultation with the local communities that have concerns over the development of the gas terminal and the impact that this may have on their lives. General Manager Brian O'Cathain and the Corrib team have held several meetings with local people in County Mayo to answer their questions and are working closely with local authorities to address these issues.
>
> The process of consultation and engagement is an ongoing one and requires a genuinely open perspective to listen to views that may not be in concurrence with our own. At Enterprise we intend to continue developing this position and adapting our approach to accommodate, wherever possible, the concerns of others. In building a profitable business and providing value to our shareholders, we are committed to protecting the environment and value the views of our stakeholders (www.entoil.com 18.05.01).[2]

However, these claims can be contrasted with community perceptions that the company was actually involved in an empty ritual or a sound-bite approach to talking.

> Their 'road-show' was a glossy production—here's a picture of the pipe, of the terminal . . . There was no counterbalance to this (interview, local resident, Pollathomas, March 2001).

> Throughout this planning process EEI . . . has behaved in a standard multinational corporation manner. The 'consultative process' which began in McGrath's public house, Pollathomas, in June 2000 could more properly be called an exercise in public relations on behalf of the consortium. I attended the meeting, signed a register, submitted a short list of questions and from that day to this have received no acknowledgement whatsoever (submission to Mayo County Council, June 2001).

---

2 Enterprise Energy Ireland (EEI) was the name of the Corrib developers up until 2002 when Shell bought a controlling stake in the consortium.

A letter sent by a number of residents to Coillte in April 2001 offers an understanding of the community's views on consultation:

> It is not consultation to meet, and listen and then proceed to ignore every-thing that has been said, and this is what has happened: there has been no discussion, no unravelling of issues.

The contrast drawn here is between 'presentation' (preferred by the company) and 'unravelling' (preferred by the community). The first approach is predictable in terms of the time it will take, the second is uncertain and open-ended.

How to belong

Similar cultural and discursive differences arise on the question of be-longing. Shell's website claims community membership:

> We never forget that we are part of a local community. We have a long history of supporting community initiatives, particularly projects which promote youth, enterprise and education (shell.com/Ireland April 2008).

But the community's view of what constitutes belonging and par-ticipation appears far more deep-rooted:

> People help each other out on a casual basis . . . People going past, who I've never seen before, if you need a hand, they'll call in and then spend half a day . . . There are real bonds there among people (interview with resident, Pollathomas, Jan. 2001).

The company's adherence to local conventions of behaviour and courtesy were perceived as pro-forma and inauthentic.

> So they kind of used one neighbour off against the next. Coming here to my door saying well we've been at your neighbour's, and coming to them and saying they were at us. This is what they did. They were schooled in this. Their people were trained in how to react to people and how to work on people's minds that this is what they did. The psychology training that the company had was unreal. One example was when they first came to the area they would wave or salute you. Now, in our area people driving along the road always salute each other. It was a custom around here. Now we were seeing complete strangers from other countries salute us as though they lived here all their lives. Of course they tried to become native! This is the same company who asked the courts to jail the men (Mary Corduff, in Garavan, 2006a: 21–2).

In this respect, Shell's claims to community membership struck the community as shallow and forced so that a veneer of artificiality was conveyed by their efforts to 'belong'. This, of course, was the opposite of what the company intended.

Conflicting timescales for judging benefits

Finally, the question arises of the time period by which to determine benefits.

> Enterprise Energy and its partners will work together with local interests to ensure that the benefits of the development are shared with the local community. We believe that the project will aid the development of improved electricity supply in the West of Ireland, therefore stimulating local businesses. In addition, the development of the Corrib gas field will encourage development of industry in the Western region and attract inward investment into the area (advertisement, *The Western People*, 8 August 2001).

Community activists sought to expose and critique the implicit time scales and values contained in Shell's statement. The lifespan of the Corrib gas field was expected to be 20 years. The community's view was that the perceived environmental damage caused by so transient a project was not justified in the long term.

> The sustainable development of Erris is only possible in the cultural, socio-economic context of a pristine environment with a history of human habitation spanning five millennia. I would respectfully draw your attention to the awful incongruity of proceeding with the Corrib Gas Project, as currently proposed, within the confines of this special place for no perceived rationale other than that of share-holder gain . . .
>
> A core value of indigenous peoples . . . is a connection to Place which is indistinguishable from People. In an area where every field, pathway, river, stream, pool, inlet and rock has a name, the abuse of Place which we have witnessed to date has been physically, emotionally and spiritually painful. I have seen grown men with tears in their eyes watch the heart-breaking attempts of four sand martins flying at the empty space where their nests, with young, had been—prior to annihilation by Shell contractors (Harrington submission, An Bord Pleanála Oral Hearing, Ballina, December 2002).

An interesting example of this cultural incomprehension occurred when the gas developers first came onto Willie Corduff's land. They pointed to a field that had taken him years to reclaim from bog.

> Then he said, 'you know why I'm here'. I said, 'not really'. 'Ah well, you've probably heard about the gas'. 'Yeah', I said, 'but I didn't think it had any-

thing to do with us. I thought it was on the other side of the estuary it was coming'. 'Well, we're not sure yet', he said, 'we're doing surveys to see which is the best option. Why I'm here is to show you where we're going to dig trial holes'. So now, I thought, he's here to show me. I thought in my own mind if it was me that was in your shoes I'd be inclined to ask you. To ask permission from you first, at least. But he didn't. He said he was here to show me.

So I kind of played along with him. He talked out there for a while and took me down to the shed over there and the field over there from the house. That had been reclaimed and it had been reclaimed over a long time with a spade. It hadn't been level but a year before that we had ploughed it up and levelled it a bit. It was cut earlier in the year and the grass was growing back lovely and green in it. So he went over to the fence and said, we'll be digging trial holes in there. I didn't say yes or I didn't say no. Yeah, just in there, he said. We'll do no damage to it, he said. He said it's a good dry field (Willie Corduff, in Garavan 2006a: 22–3).

Very important community conventions regarding land, courtesy and time were being transgressed here.

Though time was a key concept and concern informing local interpretations of the project, this would have been very difficult to express as a central issue in the public campaign. To emphasise the recovery or defence of time might lead to charges of irrelevance or even irrationality. Yet it is possible to re-imagine sustainability and the environment around time reclamation. We could argue that to solve our environmental problems we need new time horizons or time regimes more attuned to earth or geological time than to our single lifetime mode of measurement. We could argue that one of today's key social issues is the recovery of free time and leisure time outside the control of the industrial system.

Conclusion

We can see in these examples from the Corrib gas conflict how each side struggled to make sense to the other. Yet though the result may be mutual incomprehension and arguing past each other this does not lead to stalemate or paralysis in decision-making. This is because the decision-making process largely favours the corporate/'rational' view of the world (see Peace, 1993).

We need to recognise that public debate is not like a discussion between two people. The false analogy of two speakers suggests that each side knows its own position, has clear and understandable points to make, is willing to argue and to listen, is engaging in dialogue as a relative equal and has the capacity to change its own and the other's mind. Our public debates are nothing like that. Rather, in the case of campaigns, we have competing community, corporate and state actors, each characterised by internal dissent, disagreement and compromise. Individuals are often cast in the role of mouthpieces and representatives of aggregated views with which they do not necessarily entirely agree. Campaigns in turn must excavate and reveal their position as they proceed in light of new knowledge, interlocutors and settings. Debate becomes too easily a proxy war with language deployed as weapon rather than illumination. Rarely do participants change their mind, rarely do they acknowledge the superiority of the other's argument, rarely do they speak of their own doubts and uncertainties.

As was noted above, campaigns, social movements and civil society actors of all kinds are battling not just entrenched forms of power held by particular actors, but also convention, 'normality', 'commonsense', even constructed forms of rationality. They are attempting to make new claims, new ways of seeing the world and this requires a new language, one that is not ensnared in contemporary cultural practices and assumptions that force us to see the world in a particular way. So we need a new language of politics, one that can celebrate and articulate 'aliveness'. After all, we are not just self-interested, utility-maximising, rational economic actors, we are also perplexed, inquisitive, grooming, social simians!

Section III
The state and civil society: dialogue or control?

CHAPTER 8

Community development, the Irish state and the contested meaning of civil society

Martin Geoghegan and Fred Powell

Introduction

In this chapter, we examine the relationship between civil society and the Irish state through the prism of community development. We begin by exploring the theoretical context of community development, enquiring into its contested meaning. Without exhausting the totality of these meanings, we identify three community development strategies that have been pursued in the Irish context—local development, social partnership and community action. We argue that each strategy is politically infused, particularly in relation to the presumed meaning of civil society, and discuss the assumptions underpinning each strategy. We then explore the relationship between the Irish state and community development over the last 20 years or so, the period dominated by the social partnership social policy paradigm. Following the earlier exploration of the contested meaning of civil society, we discuss the social partnership policy paradigm in terms of how the state and civil society actors have related to it over that period. Based on original and secondary research, this analysis leads into a concluding discussion on the outcomes of this contested political relationship.

Community development strategies

Community development is, 'like the camel, easier to describe than define' (Powell and Geoghegan, 2004: 18). Popple (1995: 4) has observed that 'the term community work is likewise a contested concept and there is no universally agreed meaning'. The difficulty in defining community development stems from the fact that any attempt at definition implies a normative purpose to community development.

As its purpose is contested, then essential definition becomes impossible. However, what can therefore be said is that community development is a form of politics, and as such we prefer to define it in those terms. For us, community development is a form of politics whereby citizens participate in civil society through communicative action in order to directly socialise policy issues. A consequence of this definition is that civil society and the state, in the words of Kirby (2008) 'mutually constitute one another', where citizens attempt to influence the state—and vice versa—in the process of policy formation and execution. In this mutually constitutive relationship, there are many strategic options available to the actors involved, indeed so many as to make a complete typology an impossible task. However, with the benefit of a socio-historical review (see Powell and Geoghegan, 2004), we can distil three main community development strategies. Table 8.1 describes these strategies.

Table 8.1: Community development strategies

Strategy	Local development	Social partnership	Community action
Focus	Community capacity building	Local leadership development in policy-making process	Mobilisation for societal transformative change
Goals	Citizen participation	Building consensus for economic regeneration	Consciousness raising
Tactics	Negotiation	Incorporation	Conflict
Politics	Democratic pluralist	Corporatist	Ethnic groups' rights, green, Marxist, feminist, human rights

Whilst much could be said on each of these three strategies, we must limit ourselves here to brief descriptions. The local development strategy is a traditionalist, socially conservative approach to social policy that stresses notions of spatiality, place and geography, in order to reinforce an emphasis on community self-reliance rather than universalist social welfare. Its historical forebears are to be found in the co-operative movements of the 19th century, the University Settlement Movement, Muintir na Tíre, (latterly Community Councils) and the Social Service Councils of the 1960s and 1970s (Powell and Geoghegan, 2004). In theoretical terms, this view of community development relies on a view of civil society that sees it as the site of the production of 'social capital'. Skidmore and Craig (2005: 17) assert that 'social capital is an appealingly simple proposition: the kinds of social relationships people have with one another and the trust and shared values that emerge from them, influence the capacity of communities to work together to tackle common problems'. Whilst traditionalist and historically related to Catholic social teaching, this approach shares some aspects of contemporary neo-liberal social policy, tending as it does to stress the 'hollowing out' of the welfare state whilst promoting self-reliance, albeit in local community terms in addition to the emphasis on the individual.

The social partnership strategy envisages a corporatist model of social policy based upon co-operation between government, market and civil society. Jones and Novak (1999: 83) note that partnership in the UK casts the state in the role of facilitator for the market and that it is essentially 'a partnership with big business and few people else'. Betty Reid Mandell (2002: 83) shares this view of partnership, which she links to the 'New Public Management' strategy and similar policy approaches in other English-speaking countries. Critics of social partnership in Ireland such as Kieran Allen (2000) argue that social partnership in Ireland has been used to distribute wealth by stealth to the rich and to co-opt dissenting voices. However, proponents point out that social partnership has played a key role in the economic regeneration of local areas affected by market failure, notwithstanding unequal stakeholder influence.

The community action strategy conceives of community development within civil society as an activist realm that exists in tension with, but extraneous to, both formal politics and the market. Community action is a method employed by civil society organisations that seeks to change policy decisions by altering the balance of power. The National Pilot Projects to Combat Poverty during the 1970s, which adopted a Freirean approach to anti-poverty strategy, are an impressive example of this approach. The government's decision to close the programme in response to its radical agenda testifies to its effectiveness and its structural orientation towards poverty, evoking the US War on Poverty in the 1960s. This view places the state under great scrutiny, and particularly the neo-liberal agenda of the last 20 or so years. It critiques the state and its reliance on the neo-liberal market in terms of its inability to redeem promises of equality, its tendency to develop overweening bureaucracy, its inability and/or unwillingness to redistribute wealth and eradicate poverty, its reluctance to extend full citizenship to an array of marginalised groups as diverse as, for example, women, the disabled, asylum-seekers and ethnic minorities, and its recent tendency to erode on a slow but inexorable basis established civil, social and political rights such as the right to association, the right to collective bargaining and the right to peaceful protest. It is also strongly critical of the primacy afforded to the market and the attendant paring back of the welfare state.

Having described these three broad community development strategies, we now turn to the interaction of these various approaches to community development over the last 25 or so years. During this period, all of these strategies have been in evidence; however, they have been subsumed within the social partnership strategy—where state local development initiatives and civil society community action perspectives have had to operate within the hegemonic discourse of social partnership. The extent of this hegemony is where our analysis begins.

The emergence of social partnership

The ubiquity of the notion of social partnership within Irish political discourse and practice is remarkable. It has underpinned the national agreements that have been purportedly responsible for the remarkable transformation of the Irish economy, where social partnership is deemed to be the rapprochement of sectoral interests in the interests of national socio-economic development. Social partnership is also the core idea behind the reorganisation of local democracy structures, structures that now proactively draw in not just elected representatives, but also community and business representatives. Furthermore, it underpins many localised socio-economic development initiatives under the aegis of the Department of Community, Rural and Gaeltacht Affairs, including the Local Development Social Inclusion Programme (LDSIP) and the Community Development Support Programme (CDSP). Social partnership is also the organising idea in almost all other recent social development programmatic interventions such as the Department of Justice, Equality and Law Reform's Youth Diversion Projects, or Community-Based Drugs Initiatives, where elected representatives, state agencies, community groups and institutionalised civil society actors formulate and implement local public policy. Social partnership is therefore embedded in Irish political structures, the development of public policy and the implementation of that policy. In short, Ireland is a paradigmatic case of a 'partnership society' and is unique in European terms. In a recent pan-European study, social partnership was defined as the 'co-determination of public policy by governments, employer organisations and trade union confederations' (Compston, 2002: 4). However, for Ireland, the definition had to be amended in order to reflect the inclusion of civil society as a 'pillar' of social partnership, and where the relationship between the state and civil society has been codified in Green and White Papers (Ireland, 1997, 2000).

Such is the extent of social partnership in Irish public policy. The fundamental question that arises in partnership governance in terms of community development is the nature of the relationship between the state and civil society. In order to assess this relationship, we should begin with an understanding of the state. States are not unitary actors with clear roles and functions. Rather they are an 'amorphous complex of agencies with ill-defined boundaries, performing a variety of not very distinctive functions' (Schmitter, 1985, cited in Hay, 1999: 320), which generally act within the possibilities made available to them by the parameters of previous state projects. This holds until there is a crisis, when new discursive and material developments allow for new forms of material action and new ideational discourses. In the Irish case, this crisis came in the 1980s. Ireland was characterised not only by high levels of unemployment, but also by fiscal disarray and a return to mass emigration. Inflation between 1982 and 1987 averaged 20.5 per cent. GNP fell during the early 1980s, and public debt spiralled out of control, being leveraged against GNP at the staggering level of 129 per cent by 1986 (MacSharry et al., 2000, cited in Taylor, 2005: 12). These circumstances led to voter dissatisfaction and a series of collapsing political coalitions. The crisis was not solely economic: it was one of political legitimacy, where the state could not confidently act and be assured of the support of the citizenry. This, of course, was not unique to Ireland. Many western democracies were still reeling from the 1973 oil crisis and what Offe (1984) referred to as the mounting contradictions of the welfare state that had created a crisis of ungovernability. Other states had addressed this through ruptures with the existing political order, with neo-conservatism (as it was still called then, neo-liberalism as we would call it now) emerging in Thatcherite Britain and Reaganite USA. Ireland, however, with its legacy of post-independence nationalist politics, its eschewing of European left-wing/right-wing political divides that characterised politics in the age of modernity and its inclination towards subsidiarity and corporatism, addressed this crisis through new institutional logics that gave rise to a new policy-making paradigm—social partnership. On this period's impact on civil society, Larragy comments, referring to the community and voluntary sector i.e. civil society: 'Its inclusion in the process of national level social partnership can be fruitfully explored in the context of a crisis for the political elite and for liberal representative politics in the face of a deepening social malaise' (Larragy, 2006: 3).

We next explore how the state and civil society actors oriented themselves towards this new policy paradigm.

Civil society orientation

In beginning discussion of the manner in which civil society organisa-tions undertaking community development have oriented themselves to the social partnership policy paradigm, it is useful to look at how these groups typically organise and how they understand their work. This is done in order to see beyond the standard interpretation of social partnership as a 'consensus' model of social organisation, by at-tempting to theorise in political terms how civil society actors factor the social partnership paradigm into their world view and subsequent actions. In doing this, we adapt terms from Young (2000) in her ex-plication of civil society within her treatment of inclusion and de-mocracy. We argue that civil society community development groups are organised along two axes: the first we may term the 'private–civic associative orientation' and the second the 'political associative orien-tation'. Within the composite term 'private–civic', we use 'private' to denote that groups are primarily organised to meet the self-defined, self-developmental needs of participants. It is 'private' as it is par-ticularistic and inward looking. However, we qualify this description with the addendum 'civic' since, whilst this aspect is heavily oriented towards regular participants, it is rarely circumscribed by membership (or other such exclusive mechanisms, such as gender or familial ties), and is therefore theoretically open to all within the civil population. In practice though, those outside the immediate defining boundary—whether spatial or identity-based—rarely call on this inclusive policy.

This private–civic associative component of community development groups is internally oriented towards 'capacity-building', where people self-organise in a collective egalitarian manner in order to meet their felt human needs, needs emerging from their situated concerns within poor working-class or rural communities, or marginalised identity-based communities. These activities can, and do, take multiple forms— including the development of personal social services, community education, training and skills development, and many more.

The second axis is the political associative orientation. As Young has argued, '[p]olitical association is distinct from both private and civic association, in that it self-consciously focuses on claims about what the social collective ought to do. Political activity consists in voicing issues for public debate about what ought to be done, what principles and priorities should guide social life, what policies should be adopted, how the powerful should be held accountable, and what responsibilities citizenship carries' (Young, 2000: 162–3). For civil society community development groups, the political associative dimension takes the form of a civic republicanism that asserts the importance of 'ordinary' citizens taking part in the political process through direct participation, which may be described as making radical pluralist claims on that political process. This is a classical political doctrine that people have returned to during a period characterised by Barber (1984) as 'thin democracy'. This aspect is oriented towards political society and especially to local democratic structures including County/City Development Boards (CDBs), and Strategic Policy Committees (SPCs) and contains claims on both political society and the state for social inclusion. Taken in combination, these elements give us the public face of civil society community development groups, which, we argue, is best described as a civically-oriented welfarist movement. At the core of their activities is a concern with addressing poverty, social justice, social inclusion, and citizen empowerment.

State orientation

The state's orientation to the social partnership paradigm in relation to community development is best described as multi-dimensional. It is organised along four main planks: the first is the overall national policy framework in relation to community development. The most important of these are the White Paper *Supporting Voluntary Activity* (Ireland, 2000); the Taskforce on Active Citizenship; and what have been termed 'flanking initiatives' such as the National Anti-Poverty Strategy. The second is direct programmatic support to civil society community development groups through the Community Development Support Programme and the Local Development Social Inclusion Programme. The third plank is the manner in which local democracy structures have been reorganised to allow for some direct participation of civil society groups.

These developments have included the establishment of County/City Development Boards, Strategic Policy Committees, community fora as purported expressions of deliberative democracy. The fourth and final plank has been the process of modernising local governance through initiatives such as the Strategic Management Initiative, *Better Local Government,* and *Delivering Better Government*, which have given a policy basis to increased local government interaction with civil society, and to the improvement of its services through increased efficiency, whilst also providing for a greater scope of engagement than it has enjoyed heretofore.

Whilst the orientations to social partnership for civil society community development groups and the state are therefore very different, the approaches overlap in terms of points of interaction: within programmatic support programmes; within devolved social services; within local democracy; within local government. It is in these interactions that we should look to assess the relationship between the state and civil society community development groups, and it is to this analysis we now turn.

Assessing social partnership

Most discussions in relation to assessing social partnership operate at the national or international level of analysis. These analyses tend to focus on the relationship between social partnership and the reinvigoration of the Irish economy. There are important accounts that discuss the 'winners' and 'losers' during this period, and others still that look at the impact on the nature of Irish democracy during social partnership. For example, the OECD credits social partnership with being responsible for the emergence of the erstwhile 'Celtic Tiger' economy. Sabel has lauded it as 'democratic experimentalism' (Sabel, 1996). Conroy, in an early assessment of partnership arrangements, enthused about its potential in tackling long-term unemployment (Conroy, 1994: 126-127). The government has argued that it has been responsible for effectively eradicating poverty through the National Anti-Poverty Strategy (see Powell and Geoghegan, 2004: 72–113). Other commentators have been more critical. Nolan et al. (2000) argue that economic vibrancy through industrial relations stability and increased competitiveness dominates social partnership to the detriment of social inclusion and equality. Crowley has argued that social unrest has been co-opted and controlled through the 'all together' ideology of social partnership (Crowley, 1998: 69–82). Allen's (2000) Marxist account of social partnership is also highly critical. Kirby (2002) has argued that social partnership has been a means by which the state quelled social unrest through the development of consensus politics, whilst ushering in neo-liberal economic policies including a lowered commitment to welfare. The present authors have argued elsewhere that social partnership has drawn the community and voluntary sector into a project of reinvented governance (see Powell and Geoghegan, 2004).

However, whilst policy outcomes at a national level may be objectionable from the perspective of the community and voluntary sector, it remains an open question whether this is as a result of systematic marginalisation or simply the residue of globalisation and the policies needed to operate a successful trading economy in late modernity. To assess the relationship between the state and civil society in more depth, we need to look at arenas that are not subject to the forces of the globalised economy in the same way as state economic policy. This can be done by looking at the local level, where there is interaction in a plethora of 'partnership' structures. We will do this by examining local democracy, local government and localised community development programmatic policy. Further, we can also examine the politically infused notion of 'active citizenship'.

Community development and 'local democratic renewal'

In assessing the nature of the relationship between the state and civil society, we are drawn to a set of circumstances and initiatives that have occurred since the mid-1990s, which we will term the 'project of local democratic renewal'. This project consists of many intertwining strands, including a purported commitment to the refurbishment of local democracy in which its deliberative and participative capacities are enhanced; a commitment to making local government more responsive to the needs of its local community, and to providing services to that community in a more efficient and effective manner; and the commitment to the concept of active citizenship as a means of engaging citizens in governance—an approach that consists of reviewing citizen relationships to democracy via a Commission on Active Citizenship.

In response to *Better Local Government* (Ireland, 1996), the following structures were developed: in each city or county, a City/County Development Board (CDB) was established, each consisting of 25 members, made up of elected councillors, ex officio nominations from the local development initiatives described earlier, and the 'social partners'—a term usually denoting business and farming interests, and sometimes the 'community and voluntary sector'. The CDBs were to be spearheaded by a Director of Community and Enterprise (DCE), an employee of the local authority. A key task of these DCEs was to ensure the involvement of the community and voluntary sector.

Each CDB, working within the purported efficiencies under this new regime, was charged with developing a local development strategy that was to encompass social, economic and cultural development, through a deliberative democratic process that also used a social partnership approach. Much of this deliberative dimension was to be carried out through Strategic Policy Committees (SPCs), developed on thematic lines such as environment SPC, and economic development SPC, broadly aligned with the various competencies of the local authority. SPCs were also established on a 'partnership' basis, but with a built-in weighting that privileged elected representatives from city or county councils, who were to take two-thirds of the seats, with one third going to the remaining 'partners'. The 'partners' were to be allowed to arrive at their representation through their own procedures.

The beginning of the process of democratic renewal was very problematic; Keogan noted that the reforms were enforced 'from above' with little or no consultation with, or enthusiasm from, many of the social partners (Keogan, 2003). The state of establishing them became highly contentious, as were the structures themselves. Whilst intended to develop deliberative capacity and citizen participation, research has revealed a retrenchment of the powers of elected councillors combined with a diminution of policy-making potential for non-elected members. Forde, for example, found that 'the power that SPCs possess to make policy is fundamentally flawed' (Forde, 2005: 62) as the SPCs could only make recommendations to CDBs, many of which were not acted upon. Community and voluntary sector representation on the SPCs was small, thereby diluting its impact even before the issue of take-up by CDBs. SPCs were also chaired on an ex officio basis by elected representatives who were more 'concerned with upholding the interests of their party group within the local authority' (Forde, 2005: 62) than involving the community and voluntary sector.

Harvey's research on the treatment of community and voluntary sector representatives in these initiatives, and particularly the SPCs, points out further exclusion of the community and voluntary sector. He notes that 'participation by community structures in local social partnership has proved to be a difficult process, one posing many challenges, questions and dilemmas' (Harvey, 2002: 10) and that 'the SPC process has been described as disastrous' (Harvey, 2002: 21). Harvey continues: 'Voluntary and community sector representatives have found SPC meetings to be intimidating, bureaucratic, mechanistic and a destructive experience' where 'some community and voluntary sector representatives felt they were treated with contempt, suspicion and lack of basic respect' (Harvey, 2002: 20). This lack of respect was not only directed at community and voluntary sector representatives, but also at the democratic process, where, in the case of some of the CDBs, formal complaints were made by community representatives that 'agendas were predetermined, facilitation was poor, feedback reports were inaccurate and there was a conflict of interest when meetings were chaired by interested parties' (Harvey, 2002: 21).

These experiences match other research findings. Cosgrove and Ryder found that only 14 per cent of the community and voluntary sector groups they surveyed could say they had 'considerable influence' in SPCs, and only 6 per cent characterised their experience as 'positive' (Cosgrove and Ryder, 2001). The Community Workers Cooperative commented: 'It is difficult to see any concrete outcomes' (CWC, 2001, cit. Harvey, 2002). Powell and Geoghegan (2004) also found widespread dissatisfaction with social partnership from the perspective of the community and voluntary sector. Less than half of those asked expressed any positive regard for social partnership. Furthermore, only 5.9 per cent of community development activists could say they found working with the statutory sector a positive experience, and fewer than one in three could say they had any significant influence on partnership decision-making. Tellingly, a quarter of respondents experienced social partnership as a process of social control (Powell and Geoghegan, 2004: 189–224).

Community development and programmatic policy

As noted above, one of the other main arenas of interaction between the state and civil society in relation to community development is programmatic support. Here we wish to initially focus on the 'cohesion' process that has happened in relation to such programmatic support in recent years. 'Cohesion' is the name given to a policy enacted by the department responsible for managing the Community Development Support Programme (CDSP) and the Local Development Social Inclusion Programme (LDSIP)—the Department of Community, Rural and Gaeltacht Affairs (DCRGA). It is important also to note that the CDSP was originally under the aegis of the then-named Department of Social, Community and Family Affairs (DSCFA). However, the programme was reallocated to the DCRGA in 2002 (some 11 years after its inception). One of the consequences of this was that, institutionally, community development was severed from conceptions of welfare, and linked to the idea of place and culture. Begun in 2005, 'cohesion' aimed to cohere the various local development initiatives under unitary administrative management in the name of accountability, efficiency and cohesiveness. As the predominant view within political society and the state is to view community development as a shadow welfare state service provider, often insisting on labour market activation services to the detriment of other developmental activities, one of the consequences of the cohesion process has been to further the discursive and material reinvention of community development as consumerist welfare provision rather than developmental active citizenship. The managerialist logic of social service provision orients active citizenship away from political activism (the community action model outlined in Table 8.1) and points it towards more socially conservative conceptions of active citizenship that emphasise 'self-reliance' (the local development model outlined in Table 8.1). In turn, this then reasserts the pre-eminence of the state and elected representatives in the social partnership policy paradigm after the 'democratic experimentalism' of the early 1990s (Sabel, 1996).

This implicit diminution of a politically active community development coincided with the establishment of a Taskforce on Active Citizenship. A fusion of neo-liberal and communitarian logics was apparent in the early stages of the work of this Taskforce, as evidenced in the-then Taoiseach's launch speech which connected the idea of active citizenship to that of nationalism:

Last week, in the context of discussing the legacy of the 1916 Rising, I pointed out that Ireland has a deep tradition of active engagement by its citizens in every aspect of our national life and culture. During decades when the capacity of the State was limited by a lack of resources, it was the commitment of the Irish people that so often, formally and informally, provided social services, community leadership as well as a sporting and cultural life for our people (Ahern, 2006).

This quote is meaningful. Whilst initially linking the idea of active citizenship to a politically activist civil society, it then reinvents active citizenship as either voluntary social service provision or 'cultural' activity. In this case, the discursive device stresses a neo-liberal and nationalistic communitarian view of civil society, and is complemented by an emphasis on activities that are charitable, rather than political. Of course, whilst the quote is meaningful, it would be purely symbolic were it not for material reinforcement.

The Taskforce reported to government in May 2007. The report's content coincides with the neo-liberal and communitarian turn in social policy. This is evidenced in its treatment of three key issues: equality, political engagement, and governance issues. Whilst the report refers to 'concerns [that] exist in relation to equality', these concerns are less about inequality in and of itself, than on the communitarian concern of the detrimental impact of inequality in undermining social cohesion (Ireland, 2007: 1). This communitarian vision is then augmented with a neo-liberal view of active citizenship in relation to political engagement, which is largely equated with a voluntaristic, depoliticised notion of civil society based upon promoting social capital. When political engagement is discussed, the focus is primarily on voting rather than on broader interpretations of participative democracy. When the topic of the participatory democratic fora of local democracy is raised, the report acknowledges some of the difficulties noted earlier, but no significant changes are envisaged beyond that of 'strengthening' the community fora, which should be consulted with by public bodies. Opportunities for developing a politically participative citizenry are not pursued. The relationship between the state and civil society in terms of governance is underpinned by a neo-liberal managerialist view of social service provision:

Voluntary and community organisations were seen by many contributors as the backbone of Active Citizenship, with the ability to achieve cohesion and confidence in ways that government cannot achieve in its own way.

Encouragement for Active Citizenship requires support for these organisations in a way that ensures their effectiveness, transparency and accountability (Ireland, 2007: 9).

Taken together, these issues reveal an understanding of active citizenship coterminous with what Newman has described as the 'modernisation discourse':

> Modernisation is a discourse which sets out an agenda for change across different sectors (health, education, criminal justice, local government, the Civil Service). It also denotes a wider political transformation, involving the reform of key relationships in the economy, State and civil society. It offers a particular conception of the citizen (empowered as active, participating subjects); of work (as a source of opportunity for the 'socially excluded'); of community (non-antagonistic and homogeneous); and of nation . . . viewed in this context, the *modern* public management takes on a different inflection: it is a fundamentally political project, to which the rhetorics, narratives and strategies of managerialism are harnessed (Newman, 2000: 47, emphasis in original).

This 'fundamentally political project' responds not just to the demands of a globalised economy, but also to 'new discourses concerning the legitimacy of welfare state spending [which] have emerged at the cultural level. These have often been based on neo-liberal and communitarian thinking and have led to the active alignment of welfare states towards the market, resulting in part in the questioning of the state's role in redistribution' (Jensen and Pfau-Effinger, 2005: 1).

This has led many analysts to wonder whether the 'third sector' has been ethically and practically compromised by its absorption into governance (Hulme and Edwards, 1997; Landry and Mulgan, 1994; Powell and Geoghegan, 2004). The White Paper *Supporting Voluntary Activity* succinctly reflects the implications for community development in this process: 'a parallel development, both internationally and nationally, is a trend in recent years away from State Welfareism towards a more pluralistic system of provision, with many governments looking to the voluntary sector and to volunteers to play a larger role in the direct delivery of welfare services' (Ireland, 2000: 14). It concludes that changes in governance 'require a philosophy reflecting what is sometimes an enabling state or assisted self-reliance where local globalisation is assisted through the provision of external resources and technical assistance' (Ireland, 2000: 43).

What is emerging is a form of welfare where the ideology of neo-liberal and communitarian civil society, of community, eclipses the idea of a politically active civil society, binding social actors together in the name of the national project of 'partnership', that is, to make Ireland attractive for international investment. This 'politics of community' perspective underpins O'Carroll's argument that social partnership is 'best understood as [the] state-directed organisation of the economy in the name of the nation', where the 'ideological conflation of economy and society' occurs, in which the state is legitimated, as is the limitation of the demands placed upon it, whilst maintaining the power and health of corporate business (O'Carroll, 2002: 15).

Conclusion

The evidence is overwhelming. Since the inclusion of the community and voluntary sector in social partnership during a period of legitimation crisis, a slow but inexorable marginalisation of the direct participatory involvement of civil society in the political process has occurred, as the imperative for state and political legitimacy has declined during a period of unprecedented economic expansion. This has occurred at both the national and local levels, and has been accompanied by the discursive decoupling of active citizenship from the political sphere.

The community action orientated civil society that the state encountered in the 1970s and early 1980s, a civil society with no direct party political representation given the absence of a social democratic party in Ireland, has been incorporated into a project of reinvented governance, which has simultaneously facilitated the discursive reinvention of activism as active citizenship, but with its political orientation diminished. State support of community development emphasises social service delivery rather than community mobilisation, and is now organised through a department whose mission may be interpreted within the history of communitarian cultural nation-building, rather than by a department such as the DSCFA with its clear welfare remit. As a result, community development is linked primarily to a project of communitarian social cohesion in which social activism is marginalised whilst 'voluntary work' is valorised. Further, this contributes to the continued undermining of the legitimacy of the welfare state, whilst supporting a reassertion of a 'politics of community' which binds social actors together in a national project of economic modernisation. It is difficult not to conclude that civil society has been co-opted into a partnership governance of Irish society, where the boundaries between the state and civil society have become porous and permeable. We conclude that this is fundamentally about a contestation between opposing political philosophies: the state's fusion of neo-liberalism and communitarianism versus the civic republicanism of civil society, in which the classical doctrine of citizen political participation has been—for the moment at least—deftly sidelined.

CHAPTER 9

Institutionalising social partnership in Ireland

Deiric Ó Broin

... partnership has been amazingly institutionalised. Everybody accepts this and does business (O'Donnell, cited by Hastings et al., 2007: 211).

Introduction

As social partnership in Ireland enters its 22nd year, many questions remain to be answered about its role in the country's recent economic development and its impact on the health or otherwise of Irish democracy. Given the nature of the social partnership negotiations over the summer of 2008, the impact on social spending of the October 2008 budget and the subsequent re-emergence of street power, it is pertinent to ask how we have arrived at a juncture in public policy-making where groups supposedly 'on-side' in the partnership process have perceived themselves to be excluded from the real negotiations, and what, if any, are the consequences for the development of a more activist civil society.

For the purposes of this chapter it is helpful to examine first, the contested understandings of social partnership (section 2) and then the reasons why social partnership was accepted so readily by many of the key public policy stakeholders in Ireland (section 3). Section 4 reviews the critiques of social partnership and outlines a number of the key issues arising from these critiques. The chapter concludes with a brief review of the potential for the emergence of a more activist civil society.

Contested understandings of social partnership

In reviewing the very contested understandings of social partnership it is useful to examine both the 'maximalist' and 'minimalist' conceptualisations, in particular the positive and negative connotations associated with the maximalist conceptualisation. This section also reviews the work of two public servants and writers most associated with the Irish social partnership model of decision-making, Rory O'Donnell and Dermot McCarthy.[1]

In reviewing the relevant literature on social partnership, it is interesting to note the extent to which the Irish model is often, but not always, promoted as a clear and distinct break with modern liberal policy regimes. For example, Taylor contends that social partnership represents a 'new and developing form of governance in Ireland' (2005: 4), a form of governance that stands in 'contrast to the neo-liberal form of disengagement to be found in New Zealand, the USA or the UK' (2005: 5). Taylor further notes that many political scientists have questioned the efficacy of 'macro-political forms of bargaining' (2005: 23), in particular their compatibility with the prevailing processes of global capitalism. Yet at the same time, a number of thinkers have argued that this approach often places too much emphasis on the inflexibility of such a bargaining process. For example, House and McGrath argue that social partnership, as a model of neo-corporatism, is a 'modern miracle of governance. It goes beyond both Scandinavian and Dutch models of corporatism because it is more innovative, inclusive and institutionalised' (2004: 29). The American social theorist Charles Sabel, in a regularly cited work, argues that the 'Irish effort to foster development and welfare through new forms of public and private local co-ordination ... blurs the distinction between public and private, national and local, and representative and participative democracy' (Sabel, 1996: 9). This promotion of social partnership as a distinctively Irish approach to public policy decision-making is interesting, particularly when those applauding the approach are not Irish, but it raises some very important questions as to the extent to which stakeholders in the process have begun to believe their own press releases or believe that, to paraphrase Winston Churchill, 'it mightn't be great but it is better than everything we've tried before'. For example, according to former

---

1 Rory O'Donnell was formally Jean Monnet Professor of Business Studies in University College Dublin, Director of the National Economic and Social Council and is currently the Director of the National Economic and Social Development Office. Some commentators consider Rory O'Donnell 'the leading theorist of Ireland's social partnership' (Kirby 2001, 136). Dermot McCarthy is the Secretary-General of the Department of the Taoiseach and Secretary to the Government.

Taoiseach Bertie Ahern, 'we have engaged in an important piece of social innovation', a model that is 'being studied around the world' and 'puts men and women at the heart of economic development' (cited by Sweeney 2008:117).

On the other hand, a number of writers consider that social partnership has been profoundly detrimental to Ireland and to Irish civil society in particular. For example, Kieran Allen passionately argues that the process is inherently undemocratic and unequal. From this perspective the 'hegemony of social partnership ideology . . . masks the transfer of wealth to the already privileged sections of Irish society' (Allen, 2000: 35) and remains a myth that masked a decade of 'social vandalism' (Allen, 2000: 100). In a similar vein, Ó Cinnéide puts the case that the process is 'subversive to the Constitution' (1998: 41).

Thus, from the maximalist viewpoint social partnership is either one of the most interesting innovations in public policy that Ireland has devised or it is undermining the democratic nature of the state and facilitating the widespread redistribution of wealth from the working class to the wealthy.

The minimalist conceptualisation essentially portrays social partnership as a 'natural evolution of Irish corporatism' (Kelly, 2001: 1). Central to this understanding is that partnership's roots lie in Ireland's industrial relations negotiations in the 1970s and early 1980s. Indeed a recent study, *Saving the Future—How Social Partnership Shaped Ireland's Economic Success* (2007), is written by 'the leading industrial relations journalists who tracked the ups and downs of the period' (Hastings et al., 2007: vii). In this context, the International Labour Organisation describes the process as 'the centralized determination of wage increases through three-year collective agreements' (Baccaro and Simoni, 2004: 1). In similar vein, Kurt Jacobsen describes the process as 'an incomes bargain with trade unions' (Jacobsen, 1994: 15).

This view, in a modified form, can also be associated with Charles Haughey. He stated that, as a facilitator of the first social partnership agreement in 1987, the Programme for National Recovery, he saw himself and those involved in devising the agreement as 'neither prisoners of the left nor hostages of the right but pragmatists of the centre' (cited by O'Sullivan, 2006: 59). From this perspective, O'Sullivan and other commentators argue that to believe Ireland has developed 'a uniquely Irish economic model to equal the Asian Tigers, or the differing Anglo-Saxon and Rheinish financial systems' is a mistake (2006:

80). O'Sullivan maintains that 'at best' Ireland 'seems to have borrowed pragmatically from all codes, with the overall ethos and characteristics of the Irish economic "miracle" being largely Anglo-Saxon with some aspects of the Rheinish model cleverly thrown in' (2006: 80).

The negative aspect of the minimalist conceptualisation is put by Denis O'Hearn who asks 'What social partnership?' (1998: 13), a seemingly simple question that exposes the exclusionary element of the process, which the inclusion of representatives of civil society organisations attempted to remedy.

As can be seen, the social partnership process has evoked a very significant level of rhetoric and academic interest, and yet for many its impact remains unclear. Is it a constructive factor in 'creating the new and vibrant Ireland of today?' (Hasting et al., 2007, ix). If so, despite certain efforts at inclusive dialogue, has it also had a concurrent negative impact on the nature of democratic deliberation in Ireland? Before addressing these questions, the next section will examine why social partnership seemed to receive a warm embrace from so many stakeholders involved in public policy. Why was social partnership accepted so readily?

Embracing social partnership

Three distinct, though related, reasons stand out as to why the Irish polity embraced the social partnership model so passionately:

(1) the economic circumstances of the 1980s;
(2) the existence of a political and institutional culture that was sympathetic to corporatist/neo-corporatist solutions;
(3) the resilience of the existing state apparatus.

The calamity facing the Irish economy in the 1980s can be illustrated by the following figures. Between 1961 and 1973 the average annual unemployment rate was 4.7 per cent. By 1980 it had increased to 8.1 per cent and by 1986 to 18 per cent although it is widely accepted that the real level was significantly higher. Between 1981 and 1985 the number of unemployed increased from 91,000 to 226,000. In particular, the numbers employed in the manufacturing sector decreased dramatically—by 25 per cent between 1980 and 1987. In 1986 the national debt stood at £24 billion. This represented a 300 per cent increase since 1980 and constituted 148 per cent of Ireland's annual GNP. While the economic crisis facing the country was substantial and was a trigger to initiate a new form of public governance, what is interesting is that Ireland did not follow the neo-liberal route chosen by many other countries in the Anglo-American sphere.

This was because Ireland had concluded national agreements in the 1960s and 1970s, for example, the National Agreements in 1977 and 1978 and the National Understandings in 1979 and 1980. As O'Donnell observes, 'taking the long view we can see an evolution from tripartism, evident in the 1960s and 1970s, to partnership in 1987' (2008: 79). In addition, and in contrast to Ohmae's neo-liberal vision of a state in retreat in the face of globalising economic forces (1995), the Irish state proved to be rather resilient. Hayward notes that there are 'various interpretations as to why and how the resilience of the state persists' (2006: 6). For example, Taylor contends that many who casually dismissed a robust role for an engaged state in the new global economy 'appear to have been seduced by neo-conservative interpretations of alleged administrative failure which state that the problem facing western European capitalism has been an explosion in the institutional impediments to economic growth' (2002: 29). Smith notes that 'while strong market-oriented tendencies are apparent, counter-tendencies are also evident and indeed change in significance over time. Rather than characterising the Irish state *either* as 'neo-liberal' *or* as '"developmental/distributive"', economic policy has instead entailed elements of both' (2005: 135, emphasis in original). In this context it is sufficient to acknowledge that the state proved to be re-markably adaptable.

Table 9.1: Price and wage inflation, 1979–85

Year	Price inflation %	Wage inflation %
1979	13.2	15.7
1980	18.2	21.4
1981	20.4	16.7
1982	17.1	14.7
1983	10.5	11.5
1984	8.6	10.9
1985	5.4	8.0

Source: Tansey, 1998

Nonetheless the economic crisis of the 1980s, including inflation-ary pressures, problems with the public finances, and the increasingly adversarial nature of industrial relations (Hastings et al. 2007: 3) demanded a response. As Table 9.1 indicates, wage and price inflation were threatening the foundations of economic activity within the state.

Given the political and institutional culture permeating the institutions of the state, in hindsight it is not surprising that the response was influenced by the strongly corporatist tradition of Catholic social doctrine, for example the papal encyclicals *Rerum Novarum* (1891) and *Quadragesimo Anno* (1931).[2] Ireland was not alone in this. It is interesting to note that the government of the Weimar Republic also initiated a social partnership process to address wage and price inflation, the *Arbeitsgemeinschaft* of employers and trade unions. In the early stages of the new German republic this was a key component of the 'Weimar compromise' (Kolb, 1988: 79). In addition, the constitutional and legal environment facilitated a strongly corporatist approach. For example, Article 45 of the 1922 Constitution provided for the establishment of vocational councils and, while never activated, reflected a very strong interest in corporatist ideas, particularly those associated with Catholic social principles (O'Leary, 2000: 31). Though the corporatist provisions of the 1922 Constitution may not have been acted upon, the 1937 Constitution provided for an upper chamber, Seanad Éireann, to be established on a corporatist basis to 'serve as an adjunct to geographical democracy', i.e. the lower chamber, Dáil Éireann (O'Leary, 2000: 56).

Furthermore, a number of pieces of legislation were enacted which were clearly influenced by corporatism. These included the Vocational Education Act, 1930 establishing vocational (partnership) committees to manage vocational/technical education across the country, and the Local Government Act, 1941 which provided for local partnerships (Approved Local Committees) to deliver public services on behalf of local authorities.

On 21 July 1938 Taoiseach Éamon de Valera announced that his government was establishing a Commission on Vocational Organisation to examine how the state could be reorganised on corporatist principles. The Commission 'endeavoured to examine the entire organisation of Irish social and economic life and attempted to present a master plan for

---

2 Interestingly, Catholic social doctrine also contained a strong, and related, focus on subsidiarity but this did not receive the same attention from the key institutions of the state.

a new structure of governance for Irish society' (Morrissey, 2002: 151). Encouraging the members of the Commission, de Valera informed them that he considered 'the Commission on Vocational Organisation is the most important one since the establishment of the state' (2 March 1939). Seven months later, he again applauded the effort of the Commission members and stated: 'You need to continue your labours and, if possible, accelerate the pace of your efforts' (5 October 1939). The Commission took six years to complete its work and submitted its report to the Taoiseach on 1 August 1944. By this stage it was clear that its recommendations were going to be ignored. The Minister for Industry and Commerce, Seán Lemass, was particularly scathing in his comments: he called it 'querulous, nagging and propagandist' (21 February 1945) and decried its cynical attitude towards politicians. Some time later the civil service made its own 'retaliative response' (O'Leary, 2000: 112) and the report of the Commission was 'shelved' in April 1945 when a Dáil motion by the opposition proposing the establishment of a corporatist Council of Education was defeated by the Fianna Fáil government. It was clear that, while most politicians paid lip service to Catholic economic and social (corporatist) think-ing, they were reluctant to abandon the liberal democratic state they had established. Professor John Busteed, Professor of Economics in University College Cork, observed that 'for all our waving of Papal flags, we insist on discussing our economic problems on a purely agnos-tic platform' (cited by O'Leary, 2000: 36). The Commission's report was rejected largely because it was perceived to undermine the liberal democratic order but the language of corporatism was popularised and became an accepted component of political discourse.

Critiques of social partnership

At its most basic, social partnership is a 'mechanism for reaching a national agreement between the Irish government and the social partners: employers, trade unions, farmers and community and vol-untary groups. Pay, tax and social welfare as well as other economic and social concerns are currently agreed roughly every three years' (Cantillon et al., 2001: 318).[3] O'Donnell credits the institutions of social partnership with a central role in 'mediating Ireland's transfor-

3 This definition is taken from the glossary of terms in *Rich and Poor—Perspectives on tackling inequality in Ireland* (2001: 318).

mation from economic laggard to economic star through aligning state strategy with economic and social interests' (Kirby et al., 2002: 5).[4] In a report written for the Organisation of Economic Co-operation and Development on social partnership and social innovation, Charles Sabel writes that social partnership 'blurs the distinction between public and private, national and local, and representative and partici-pative democracy' (1996: 9).

Despite Sabel's rhetorical flourishes, the model of social partner-ship in Ireland has almost prosaic origins. It was born in the depths of economic and social crisis. Inflation, wage and price spirals, industrial unrest, unemployment, emigration, poverty and a massive government debt in the early to mid 1980s led Ireland to be viewed by many as an 'economic basket case'.[5] The key stakeholders concluded that only a competitiveness-based strategy could enable the economic and social survival of a small open economy. This consensus was arrived at through the tripartite consultative body, the National Economic and Social Council (NESC). The publication of *Strategy for Recovery* by NESC in 1986 represented a key element of this consensus. In 1987 a minority Fianna Fáil administration accepted the terms of the NESC report and convened tripartite talks that led to the first agreement, the *Programme for National Recovery*. The negotiation of the following three agreements (the *Programme for Economic and Social Progress*, the *Programme for Competitiveness* and *Work and Partnership 2000*) broadened the range of issues for discussion. The fifth programme, *Partnership for Prosperity and Fairness*, saw representation extended to a range of groups from the community and voluntary sector while the negotiation of the sixth programme, *Sustaining Progress*, saw the majority of those groups walk out.[6]

In assessing the impact of the social partnership process on Irish

---

4 These include the National Economic and Social Council, the National Economic and Social Forum, the National Council for Partnership and Performance Forum (these are now situated in the National Economic and Social Development Office) and the National Competitiveness Council (managed under the aegis of Forfás).

5 Phrase used by RTÉ current affairs programme *Today Tonight* in 1987.

6 The Community Platform, which represents 25 of the 30 community and voluntary sector organisations in the process, staged a walk-out from a plenary session in July 2002 to express their belief that the equality agenda was not being addressed.

civil society, in particular on the role of those representing marginalised groups, it is important to remember that only the most powerful interests are effectively represented. The Irish Congress of Trade
Unions, the Irish Business and Employers Confederation and to a
more limited extent the Irish Farmers Association control access to the
negotiations and are reluctant to allow access to the community and
voluntary pillar. Mary Murphy's examination of the process (2002b)
makes very clear that the problem-solving ethos of the process left no
room or inclination to challenge the status quo. The process 'both developed and reflected a shared understanding' of the issues perceived
to be in need of redress (Murphy, 2002b: 5). Unfortunately, social and
civic equity was low on the list of priorities.[7]

When examining the impact of social partnership on civil society
and particularly on those groups working to represent the interests of
marginalised groups, I have found it helpful to review the analyses of
the process by Mary Murphy (2002b) and Seamus Ó Cinnéide (1998).
The analyses share significant features and agree on a number of important issues. Ó Cinnéide contends that social partnership has effectively sidelined the legislature and that unelected stakeholders now
exercise considerable influence in the formulation of socio-economic
policy. Murphy also notes the bypassing of the legislature but, unlike
Ó Cinnéide, focuses on the concentration of power in the hands of
the executive, ably assisted by a dynamic cohort of civil servants. Both
views raise matters of concern.

Ó Cinnéide contends that the social partnership process has undermined the role of the existing elected representatives, radically
increased the power of the executive and hidden the lack of influence
of the social partners. Ó Cinnéide (1998) powerfully articulates a
cogent critique of social partnership on the grounds that it creates and
sustains a democratic deficit. He notes that the process 'represents a
major shift in power from elected representatives to full-time officials
in the civil service and the organisations of the major interests. It is,
of course, neither participative (except for a small group of activists)
nor democratic in any ordinary sense of that word' (Ó Cinnéide, 1998:

---

7 While there are differences of opinion as to the degree to which the social
partnership process sacrificed equality for competitiveness, most commentators
agree that it relegated equality. See, for example, Ó Riain and O'Connell (2000),
Kirby (2001) and O'Hearn (1998, 2001).

47). This view has been echoed by a number of TDs, most notably Róisín Shortall and Noel Ahern.[8] On 23 February 2000, in a widely noted speech made as part of a wider Dáil debate on tax individualisation, Ahern stated:

> I am concerned by us becoming irrelevant. The social partners include Community Action Network, Community Workers Co-op, Conference of Religious of Ireland, European Anti-Poverty Network, Focus Ireland, Gay and Lesbian Network, Irish Association of Older People, National Adult Literacy Agency, Irish Commission for Prisoners Overseas and so on. They are happy with the drift towards individualisation, which is interesting, but I would rather listen to my colleagues on all sides of the House. I do not know who some of those organisations represent—not many. Many of them are funded by various Ministers but I do not know who they represent. Many are set up just to represent themselves. Many Members were concerned with individualisation and I would much rather listen to a cross-section of Deputies who, for good or bad, have some sort of mandate and who represent those who have elected us. I am concerned that too much emphasis is being shifted away from the Dáil just because that motley crew has endorsed this—I wonder if they discussed it. The fact that it is in the partnership deal and makes them happy does not make me happy. It is a matter for debate among public representatives who have been elected by the people.

He went on: 'I hope that we, as elected representatives, continue to make this House relevant and discuss issues within this House rather than outside it'.

In a similar vein, on 23 October 2002, Minister Éamon Ó Cuiv responded to a question about funding and methods he would put in place to overcome the distrust that existed between the local development structures and the public representatives. He stated: 'We are the only ones elected by the people and primacy must go to those who represent the people in this parliament. Any of us who deviate from that are doing a disservice to democracy.' Central to the TDs' understanding of social partnership is that they have somehow become irrelevant to the public policy-making process. Supporting their perception is the widely held belief that no major policy decision will be taken unilaterally by the government without consulting the major social partners. For example, as the NESC put it, 'it is now inconceivable that major policy initiatives would be taken without some consultation with,

---

8 Noel Ahern is currently (late 2008) Minister of State in the Department of Transport.

and/or involvement of, the social partners and this is reflected at both national and local level' (NESC, 1999: 79).

The second criticism of the process relates to the views of organisations representing marginalised groups. Murphy notes that a major feature of the community and voluntary sector's involvement in the process has been the lack of time and resources available to criticise and campaign. She contends that 'social partnership is the vehicle through which a global policy regime of neo-liberalism has been inserted into the Irish political psyche and discourse' (2002b: 4). A consequence of the sector's participation in the process is that it has had little or no influence on shaping the agenda.[9] The kernel of Murphy's critique is her analysis of those who set the agenda, public servants. She notes that 'it is striking the degree to which the unwritten rules of the game imply that you must negotiate through civil servants and only civil servants' (2002b: 10). The major social partners agree to this as it allows the process to continue without interference from politicians. Even the Community Platform's walk out from the *Programme for Prosperity and Fairness* plenary session in July 2002 failed to influence the process in any meaningful way.

Despite differences in emphasis—Murphy's contention that the process has actually enhanced the power of the executive and Ó Cinnéide's argument that elected representatives have been sidelined in favour of unelected stakeholders—there is a substantial overlap in their views. Elected representatives in the legislature are kept removed from the process by government and by the social partners. O'Donnell concedes that it is ministers rather than party politicians that have 'close connections with social partnership' (2000: 195) but claims that this is not unusual. He contends that 'the relationship between social partnership and representative democracy is linked to the question of devolution. While Ireland has adopted an unusual approach to that question, our problem can be seen as an acute version of a world-wide problem of democracy' (ibid.).

However, Murphy's argument that civil servants appear to play a dominant role in minding the neo-liberal agenda is an interesting insight into the process. Government has maintained a huge degree of

---

9 Murphy contends that the confident manner in which the Minister for Finance introduced the regressive SSIA scheme is evidence of the lack of power of the sector.

policy autonomy and this is the key to understanding why civil servants play such a dominant role. Hardiman (2001: 305–6) notes that tax policy has never been controlled by the partnership process. A similar case arises with regard to immigration and refugee policy. Recent attempts by the social partners to raise the issue ended within minutes. Government stated that it was not up for discussion and was outside the scope of social partnership. Hardiman (2001: 307) contends that this reflects the experience of other countries and that a strong state is required to initiate, manage and sustain a strong partnership process. Since corporatist or neo-corporatist structures 'easily produce policy stalemates' government must be prepared to use the 'threat of unilateral intervention to achieve the objectives it wishes to see attained'.

Hardiman's point is important because it addresses the issues raised by politicians such as Noel Ahern TD and Éamon Ó Cuiv TD, and writers such as Ó Cinnéide. I suggest that rather than being eclipsed by unelected stakeholders, TDs' role and function as elected representatives and members of the legislature have been undermined not by community sector representatives but by the executive (in which both TDs have served).

In addition to the critiques articulated by Murphy (2002b) and Ó Cinnéide (1998), there are two other pertinent contributions. The first examines the undermining of a key component of civil society, that is, the community sector (Meade, 2005). The second addresses the fact that the consensus-oriented objectives of the process tend to devalue politics and promote a managerial view of public policy (Dillow, 2007). In relation to the undermining of the community sector, as Rosie Meade observes, 'it is now extremely difficult to distinguish between an "autonomous" community organisation and a state dependent anti-poverty vehicle' (2005: 350). As community sector representatives have engaged with the social partnership process they have been granted official recognition by government as de facto representatives of the marginalised and socially excluded. Concurrently the state has claimed that this development represents an 'enablement of civil society' and reflects a more participative strand in public policy decision-making (2005: 349). Hastings et al. similarly argue that 'social partnership enhances democracy rather than diminishes it, by giving an effective voice to social partners, and may also favour the weaker groups who, if left outside, may protest vociferously, but often quite ineffectively' (2007: 206). However, as a number of groups have found to their cost, the state's role in funding and monitoring their activities, purely to ensure the accountable expenditure of public funds, has reduced their autonomy and independence of action. Their co-option, voluntary though it may have been, has undermined their ability to advocate on behalf of those whose interests they represent.

This is disturbing as campaigning and advocacy are central to a robust civil society. The government's provision of funding to groups based on their ability and willingness to deliver public services, and to incorporate the attendant bureaucracy such as service level agreements, co-opts an important component of Irish civil society, the community sector, into a service delivery-oriented system, and inhibits its advocacy functions. In essence, the state has engaged in a process of bureaucratising potential vehicles for dissent.

Finally, a critique of the New Labour government in Britain is relevant to the relationship between civil society and the social partnership process in Ireland. As social partnership has become increasingly institutionalised, its problem-solving ethos has resulted in the devaluing of politics and the promotion of managerialism. Chris Dillow's *The End of Politics—New Labour and the Folly of Managerialism* makes the point that the big idea of New Labour was that trade-offs between conflicting values could be managed away by clever policies, that management can replace politics. In some ways this is one of the most damning critiques of social partnership—that by sidelining the legislature and thereby reducing the electorate's ability to lobby and influence matters, it has devalued politics in the broad sense. Despite the protestations of some stakeholders in the process, as social partnership has become institutionalised its ability to recognise the multiple and conflicting meanings of the ideals of equality and efficiency has been undermined.

Dermot McCarthy, a key figure in the social partnership process and its institutionalisation, provides an interesting analogy that sums up how its supporters would like the process to be perceived:

> It's like a muscle, the more it's used the stronger it gets . . . it brings people together and encourages them to be minded to solve problems, rather than to create or exacerbate them, and to do it in a way which respect parameters that everyone agrees are either necessary or desirable (cited by Hastings et al., 2007: 211).

This perspective is welcome as it openly acknowledges the problem-solving core of the process. The difficulty with the problem-solving approach, however, is that groups do not necessarily agree as to what constitutes a problem, and if they do, it is hard to prioritise how the problem should be addressed. The process undermines the political debate about values and replaces it with an argument that, since social, economic and political problems can have a mutually agreeable solution, stakeholders must engage until they devise such a solution. This not only undermines the values underpinning politics but promotes a managerialism that weakens, or may weaken, the democratic foundations of public policy decision-making. As the social partnership becomes increasingly institutionalised this represents a substantial obstacle to the emergence of a more activist civil society.

Moving towards a more activist civil society

There are a number of important lessons to be learned from the institutionalisation of the Irish model of social partnership. The first relates to the representation of socially excluded groups in the process. Mary Murphy's contention about the balance of power within the process is important. It is clear that if a model of representation is to be developed that adequately incorporates the social experiences and perspectives of socially excluded groups, then the argument made by Rosie Meade becomes increasingly important, that an independent and sustainable funding mechanism is necessary to ensure that such groups can be represented in a useful and constructive manner.

A related point concerns the exercise of power within the process. There is some evidence that traditionally excluded groups have been involved in the public policy process, but it is also clear that the power they exert within the process is very limited. This reflects to a certain extent the original conceptualisation of social partnership, since at its simplest the process was about co-opting those who could obstruct the future implementation of public policy. By involving these groups in the process, their options to advocate alternative positions outside the process were severely limited. However, representatives of marginalised groups lack the power of the employers', trades unions' or farmers' groups. They do not have the same ability to hold up the implementation of decisions agreed during the social partnership process.

In concluding, it is important to note that I do not propose that Irish civil society withdraw from engagement with the social partnership process. Instead I suggest that social partnership has deep historical and institutional roots and constitutes a key component of a resilient Irish state; this implies that it is not a simple choice of either activist politics or participation and managerialism. What is required is a clear understanding, on the part of civil society, of the social partnership process and the potential costs of being co-opted. There is a space for more critical engagement, with parameters only worked out in practice as the social partnership process, given its institutional endurance, will react to such an approach. Given the sight in autumn 2008 of 15,000 pensioners and 10,000 students marching and articulating a very different type of politics it will be interesting to see how social partnership reacts.

CHAPTER 10

Community development: a practitioners' perspective

Catherine Murray and Paul Rogers

Introduction

The collaborative approach adopted in writing this chapter has been mutually beneficial in that we were able to share experiences, observations and knowledge from both sides of the Atlantic and to identify common issues and themes. We address many of those issues and themes in this chapter, including questions about the nature of social exclusion and the role we, as individuals, play in perpetuating exclusion. In addition, we briefly examine the principles of community development and its current role in Ireland. We also explore the role of social networks within the context of developing social, economic and cultural capital[1] and query current practice with regard to the building of power in marginalised communities and groups. In addressing these issues we draw upon examples from the USA, the UK and Ireland.

It is important, however, to outline the current policy climate and challenges that impact upon community work in Ireland. Powell and Geoghegan (2004) examine many of these issues in a comprehensive study of community development in Ireland. Lee (2006) summarises the key points succinctly in *Community Development: Current Issues and Challenges*, published by the Combat Poverty Agency.

---

1 'The concept of cultural capital refers to the role that distinctive kinds of cultural tastes, knowledge and abilities play in relation to the processes of class formations in contemporary societies. It has been particularly influential in sociological accounts of the ways in which the middle classes distinguish themselves from the working classes through their distinctive cultural tastes, knowledge and competencies. It has also played a significant role in accounts of differences within the middle classes (between culturally 'rich' professionals and managers, for example)'(Open University, 2008).

Community development: current status

If there is one indication that community development has now gained credence as a suitable methodology for tackling poverty and inequality in modern Ireland, it is probably the growing acceptance[2] within statutory agencies that those experiencing marginalisation or exclusion should be brought into the decision-making process. In recognising the central role of target group representation, organisations also need to be aware that structural inequalities[3] may hinder these groups' ability to take part effectively in these processes. Thus, systems and supports should be put in place to ensure equal participation.

The acceptance of community development is also acknowledged in the proliferation of government spending aimed at tackling social exclusion. That said, an over-reliance on government spending presents significant challenges in that funding priorities are often determined by the state with local communities having little influence. Increasingly, funding is for service interventions and not for capacity building. This approach to funding is, in our view, myopic in that it drip-feeds funding into communities and ensures a dependency culture when we should be looking towards independence and long-term sustainability.

The reliance of community development on government funding is not without cost; it carries a considerable bureaucratic and administrative burden, which many groups do not have the capacity to manage, and when they do it often significantly distracts from their core activities. Additional costs arise when the ethos of a group runs counter to government interests or policy. There is the danger that funding will be pulled, as was experienced by the Community Workers Co-operative,[4] or that the role of the group will be queried, as happened to Pavee

---

2 We use the term 'growing acceptance' as one cannot assume that a commitment to community development as a process at one level within an organisation will permeate all levels of that body. In our experience many organisations face considerable challenges in ensuring community development is etched into organisation ethos and culture.

3 'Structural inequality is defined as a condition that arises out of attributing an unequal status to a category of people in relation to one or more other categories of people, a relationship that is perpetuated and reinforced by a confluence of unequal relations in roles, functions, decision rights and opportunities' (Dani and De Hann, 2008 : 3).

4 The Community Workers Co-operative was funded as a National Anti-Poverty Network. In December 2004 the co-operative was informed that core funding would be withdrawn at the end of March 2005.

Point.⁵ The question arises: if one is reliant on government funding how hard can one 'rock the boat'?

In recent times, the Cohesion⁶ process has had a considerable impact on local area partnerships. It has hindered progress and distracted attention from the complex task of building a socially inclusive society. This ongoing realignment of local development structures should in theory enhance the capacity of the sector but we should be aware that systemic change takes time and it needs to be resourced appropriately. Furthermore, it cannot be assumed that a commitment to community development as a process will be at the core of the culture and values of a complex multifarious delivery system for social inclusion. Indeed, our experience indicates that a practical commitment to community development exists close to the ground but at higher levels of the social inclusion system the commitment becomes more theoretical. Therefore the question arises: what is the role of community development in modern Ireland?

Role of community development

There is a considerable body of literature available to anyone seeking a definition of community development. Generally the core principles of community development—a developmental process based on collective action with an ethos of social justice and equality—will be reflected in some way in all definitions. The two examples quoted here are from Irish bodies but there are many international examples.

> [Community development is about] enabling or empowering people to actively work for social change which will improve the quality of their lives, the communities in which they live and/or the society of which they are a

---

5 In 2007 the then Minister for Justice, Brian Lenihan, indicated that he would re-assess government funding arrangements to Pavee Point. The rationale for this review was that the Minister was of the opinion that Pavee Point had stepped beyond their remit in supporting Roma Gypsies who were camped on a roundabout in Ballymun on the outskirts of Dublin.

6 First initiated by the Irish Government in 2003, the Cohesion process aims to extend social inclusion coverage throughout Ireland on a county by county basis. Within a rural setting this entails the merging of LEADER and Partnership companies into one cohesive organisation. Urban Partnerships are required to expand their boundaries to ensure contiguity with local authority areas. The process began with 'a comprehensive consultation process with the providers of schemes and programmes and the social partners on improving local delivery structures' (Government of Ireland, 2003).

part. It is a collective process that recognises the interdependence of people. It helps people to identify and articulate their needs, and to influence the decision-making processes and structures that affect them, their communities and wider society (Combat Poverty Agency, 2000: 3).

[Community development is about] enabling people to enhance their capacity to play a role in shaping the society of which they are part. It works towards helping groups and communities to articulate needs and viewpoints and to take part in collective action to influence the processes that structure their everyday lives' (Area Development Management Ltd., 2000: 28).

Unfortunately, in our experience the term has a tendency to mislead people into assuming it is something that it is not. What is apparent is that the state sees community development as a tool to deliver social inclusion as is evident in Chapter 11 of the National Development Plan 'Social Inclusion Priority'. Indeed, this has been the case since the government made 'social inclusion a key horizontal element of the National Development Plan 2000–2006' (NDP, 2007: 236). The question is whether it can deliver social inclusion within the constraints of the current operational landscape, government policies and a needs-based paradigm.

The Petri dish model[7]

There is no question that significant resources and initiatives have been put in place by government to tackle social exclusion. However, our experience and that of many of our colleagues has led us to question the restrictive criteria of key programmes aimed at tackling social exclusion, criteria that are set at the top and often do not fit with priorities identified by communities. Key initiatives, such as the Local Development Social Inclusion Programme and the Community Development Programme, focus resources on specific defined target groups. Funding is then delivered through these programmes to local organisations to alleviate disadvantage and in theory bring about social change.

---

7 We use this term to define restrictive practices that often develop due to strict and literal adherence to programme guidelines where initiatives and funding are delivered to marginalised groups in isolation from (a) other significant and influential social actors, and (b) the potential of the wider community to engage in social inclusion initiatives. In addition, this model often overlooks consideration of other relevant aspects impacting on communities, such as the questions of accessibility (transport) or the quality of the built environment.

Due to the restraints of the programmatic approach and the nature of disadvantage which exists in pockets, those of us who work at the coalface of exclusion often find ourselves working with groups and communities in isolation from other significant social actors. This Petri dish model ensures that the focus of excluded communities remains within their own sphere of influence and inhibits the building of powerful relationships above and beyond their immediate peers. We collectively struggle to bring about change with little or no power to do so, and with few allies beyond our peers who share our worldview. Our concern is that this model does not reflect an essential component of how society works: that is, the complex arrangement of relations that facilitate the building of social,[8] cultural and economic capital, the absence of which can severely inhibit life chances. But, before we explore these relations further let us briefly examine the nature of social exclusion.

Who does the excluding?

The concept of society as a 'complex system whose parts work together to promote solidarity and stability' (Macionis and Plummer, 1997: 23) is central to a structural-functional social paradigm. Despite its associations with social Darwinism it is a useful model to use when exploring social exclusion.

As a system, society ensures the passing on of many attributes essential to individual, collective and systemic well-being through processes such as socialisation, education, enculturation.[9] These processes are in turn facilitated through reciprocal relationships between individuals, groups and organisations or formal and informal networks. To benefit as an individual from this system there is a compelling need to conform or comply with the normative values inherent within the system. To do otherwise would run the risk of exclusion. But who is doing the excluding? 'One hears about "the marginalised", and the "socially excluded", but there is little discussion of who is excluding or marginalising them. It seems to be a process with no active subjects' (Allen, 2000: 37).

---

8 'In the political science, sociological, and anthropological literature social capital generally refers to the set of norms, networks, and organizations through which people gain access to power and resources, and through which decision making and policy formulation occur" (Grootaert, 1998: 2).

9 Enculturation is the process of acquiring the knowledge, behavioural expectations, norms, and values associated with one's particular ethno cultural group.

It is important to note that the system itself cannot exist without the individuals that make it up and it is reliant upon them to ensure its continuation. This is not to deny the powerful forces that ensure system equilibrium is maintained. Nevertheless, one cannot ignore the role of the individual in perpetuating the system. Where a system excludes it is individuals within that system that perpetuate the exclusion. In essence it is you and I who exclude. We do this by maintaining the cultures, ideologies and belief systems essential to its maintenance, the modes and patterns of behaviour we have adopted, the little distinctions we make in our encounters with others, and the decisions we make every day.

There is no doubt that education plays a key role in enabling individuals to develop an understanding of the processes that shape both themselves and their society. However, it is easy to remain cosseted in one's worldview and aloof from the dire circumstances of others unless one has lived the experience of exclusion or has the tools to empathise. Thus, education needs to be tempered with experience if individuals are to emerge with a level of self and societal awareness that will enable them to rise above the need to conform and perpetuate exclusion. If social change is a goal of community development then a key element of transformation must rest within the hearts and minds of the individuals that make up society.

As practitioners, we are faced with the realisation that, despite a significant commitment to social inclusion, there is little evidence that this commitment has become part of the dominant culture and ethos of many statutory bodies and other organisations working with a social inclusion remit. It may be stated in strategic plans or mission statements but it is not necessarily reflected in the value systems of organisations or individuals within the organisations. This is a cause for concern, as true and lasting social change will not take hold until the prevailing beliefs with regard to those experiencing exclusion are challenged and individuals have an opportunity to develop a deeper understanding of exclusion.

It must be acknowledged that, in addition to direct funding of work with defined target groups, the government also develops policies and legislation to stimulate social change and influence behaviour, for example the Equality Act 2004. Such legislation is extremely important in that it acknowledges inequality in society and enshrines moral values. Yet legislation is a blunt tool in terms of influencing social change. It can modify individual behaviour but it may not change attitudes or beliefs. And it is the changing of attitudes that will bring about real and meaningful social change. To facilitate this it is imperative that we move away from the isolationist or Petri dish model and develop a model that generates interface opportunities between those excluding and those experiencing exclusion. A model is needed that enables the growth of understanding based on humanist values and the building of relationships between those that experience exclusion and those in positions of power. Indeed, to truly bring about social change 'we need both cultural transformation and government action—a change in values and a change in policy—to promote the kind of society we want' (Obama, 2006: 63).

Thus the question arises, how can we as community workers facilitate a growth in understanding or initiate a shift in values and attitudes that will bring about an inclusive society? How can we raise the moral bar when the locus of our energy is often confined exclusively within target groups? In addressing these questions, we cannot ignore the need to build power and bridge the social divide. This brings us back to the role of social networks in building social, cultural and economic capital.

The slumbering giant and the anthill

A key question that vexes many community workers and activists is what makes some groups powerful and some weak? How is it that one geographic area can have enormous levels of community activity on the ground, albeit activity that reflects social deprivation, yet wield little or no power? In contrast, some areas appear to be slumbering, there may be little evidence of community activity on the ground yet the community may wield significant power. For example, in 2005 Fingal County Council was about to begin work on a pumping station for a sewage treatment plant in a coastal park in a middle-class estate in Balbriggan, north County Dublin. Despite 'consultation' with the community, there was little awareness of the planned development until the morning construction work was due to start. One woman noticed that a JCB was about to start digging in the park and went over to enquire from the driver as to what he was doing. Upon hearing about the pumping station she called her neighbours and a blockade was established. Within two days this small group had linked with other people through social networks and enlisted support from a number of connected people including a diplomat and a famous Irish comedian. The resultant media flurry, DIPLOMAT RAISES STINK OVER SEWAGE STATION (T. Hogan in *Fingal Independent*, 2005), forced Fingal County Council to reassess its plans and within a short period of time an acceptable solution was agreed.

What is interesting about this example is that this community has little in the way of physical assets that would indicate a community exists at all. There is no local community centre, youth service, or other such services. The real asset of the community that helped it to influence Fingal County Council was its social capital, an asset that enabled it to mobilise those with influence within the community and to link to others with power beyond the community. In this case the power of a comedian and a diplomat to attract media attention and thus amplify the voice of the community was a crucial asset.

This campaign was a grassroots reaction from a community that was slumbering. Yet it had the wherewithal to mobilise and reach out beyond itself. It is a simple example of community action, not to be confused with the process of community development, yet it shows that we cannot afford to overlook the power of allies and networks. Influential groups wield significant power in the form of capital, be that economic, social or cultural. They have access to strong and powerful social networks and thus are in a position to influence thinking and modify behaviour. They have the capacity to motivate individuals and organisations in ways that excluded groups could only dream of. This story illustrates the crucial role that networks play in mobilising communities and creating change.

Society works through networks

If the ultimate goal of community development is to bring about positive social change, we need to increase the power of excluded communities and individuals by building strong alliances with other significant social actors. In order to accomplish this, we must understand the nature and type of relationships that contribute to the formation of formal and informal networks. In particular, we must focus on two types of relationships: public and private.

Public relationships are formed with a variety of people in everyday life, and often with some form of motivation in mind. Usually, both parties have something to gain from the relationship. That is not to say that all public relationships are based on self-interest, often they are initiated to achieve some task or collective goal. As practitioners of community development, 'we also see actions—day in and day out—that reflect values which have clear social components that take us well beyond the narrow confines of purely selfish behaviour' (Sen, 1999: 261). Public relationships consist of the following: professional associations, boards of management, work/business relationships, parishes, the schools our children or we attend, political parties, and organised community groups. It is most likely that such relationships will be formed with people who are different to ourselves in terms of background or education. Thus public relationships directly affect the strength of formal networks as they facilitate bridging between groups. They are 'where we learn about making and keeping public promises, and about how to hold and be held accountable' (Chambers, 2003: 73).

Private relationships are mostly permanent, and are more likely to exist between people who share similar backgrounds. One of the main needs met by these relationships is that of being liked and accepted. They 'are foundational and inform all others. The small circle of private relationships typically includes self, spouse, children, extended family and a very few close friends' (ibid.). Occasionally there is a blurring of the distinction between the private and the public. Some relationships can move fluidly from one type to the other and back again, depending on circumstances. As public relationships constitute formal networks, informal networks arise from private relationships. The creation of strong relationships is essential to growing social networks—and it is through these networks that communities can build power and power-ful allies. However, to utilise such networks fully communities must map them, understanding their strengths and their degree of economic and social capital.

The 'right' social capital

Frequently, marginalised communities do not have the social capital that wealthy communities possess and therefore struggle to make their issues public and have a real say in social change. As noted earlier in our example of community action, some communities have the capac-ity to 'punch above their weight' in terms of mobilisation and efficacy when an issue arises. This is a result of their strong formal and informal networks that facilitate access to high levels of social, cultural and economic capital. If we continue to work with groups in the Petri dish model, there is a danger that we will perpetuate the development of bonding social capital—which is a form that 'brings people together who already know each other' (Gittell and Vidal, 1998: 15). To increase power we need to create or seek opportunities to develop bridging social capital, a form of social capital that 'brings people together who previously did not know each other' (ibid.).

Given the nature of the neighbourhoods targeted by community development workers or the government, without links to outside resources and opportunities, the stronger ties developed internal to the communities might not be efficacious because they would lack links to outside resources and opportunities. This would make it more difficult to motivate and sustain community development activity (Gittell and Vidal, 1998: 15–16).

Thus if we are to create lasting social change, we cannot afford to ignore the role of bridging social capital. We must seek ways for communities to form bridging relationships with other more powerful social actors. For example, in 2008 Dublin City University opened an outreach centre in Ballymun, a disadvantaged community on Dublin's northside. This centre, called 'DCU in the Community', offers a variety of different educational opportunities for local residents and staff. The result of this initiative is not only an increase in access to third-level education, but also the formation of bridging relationships between people. People from a variety of socio-economic backgrounds, ethnicities and ages all come together in this centre for the common purpose of learning. This has the potential to increase the power of individuals and the community of Ballymun through the formation of strong public relationships and the building of allies beyond the community.

Another example of the importance of 'bridging' can be seen in the experience of a group of formerly homeless tenant leaders in Chicago, now living in properties owned by the national, non-profit organisation, Mercy Housing Lakefront. This group worked on a campaign to increase community safety outside a local shop where their fellow tenants were being harassed, intimidated, mugged, and offered drugs. The leaders approached their goal of increasing safety through the 'crime triangle' model. The three sides of the triangle were location, victims, and offenders. The tenant leader group produced a strategy that focused on each side of the triangle. Through their work, they developed a close relationship with the local police, and began to attend monthly community policing meetings. Prior to this involvement, some of the tenant leaders were hesitant about working with the police, due to negative past experiences and, for the African-American members of the group, some upsetting experiences of racial profiling. Steadily, over a period of eight months, the formerly homeless tenants gained the respect of the police officers and a strong relationship developed between them, built on open communication and trust.

In addition, the leaders built relationships with the store manager, workers, and the owners of other stores in the area. They also worked with their neighbours, some of whom had negative perceptions of homeless people. Over time, the mainly white, highly educated neighbours began to look to the formerly homeless leaders to set the agenda. The two groups exchanged information and worked together but, most importantly, relationships were built and stereotypes were broken down. The end result was not only a lessening of crime at the corner store, but an increase in the leaders' social capital. The formerly homeless leaders built strong public relationships with people outside their regular peer group, and helped to strengthen the community as a whole.

Economic capital

In addition to the development of strong social capital communities must also have access to real economic capital that enables them to generate income and prioritise where this income should be spent. One example of how this could be done is drawn from the experience of the former residents of Eldon Street in Liverpool.[10]

The Eldonians have had great success in the regeneration of their area through the transfer of physical assets and the development of community-led management structures. They 'established a vehicle to enable the community to participate fully in the regeneration of the area, based upon three separately constituted bodies' (The Eldonians, 2007: 23). A parent company called the Eldonian Community Trust Limited has overall responsibility for strategic development and planning. It has over 600 members and its business is handled by two subgroups, the Eldonian Community-Based Housing Association Limited, responsible for housing development and management, and

---

10 The development model in the UK tends to focus on long-term sustainability with a focus on community-based assets.

the Eldonian Group Limited, which manages economic regeneration and looks after community-based businesses. Through these groups, the Eldonians exercise real power within their community and have significant control over key assets and resources and access to independent income streams.

If a similar approach was taken in Ireland, and additional funding was directed towards helping communities purchase and develop physical assets, groups could reduce their dependence on government funding and begin to direct resources in a manner that reflects the unique potential of their community and the challenges they face.

Agitation for organic change

In addition to increasing social and economic capital, it is imperative that community development is driven from a 'grassroots' perspective. From our observations, the Irish government plays a major role in determining the programmes and goals of community development. Sometimes ideas or issues that communities wish to address do not fit into the 'box' of programmatic funding. Thus, it is quite possible that programmes and bureaucracy hinder grassroots initiatives and consequently community participation.

With access to strong social and economic capital, communities may be far better placed to bring about organic change. For example, the community-organising model that is used in the US depends on work being determined by local leaders, and then supported by staff; in theory this should be happening on the ground in Ireland. 'To be fully participatory, the agenda needs to be set by the communities involved, rather than outside agencies deciding upon the priorities to be addressed and then working with local people to achieve them' (Willis, 2005: 104). In the previous example from Chicago, the community organisers and leaders ran their campaign using an 'action for change' model where the leaders determined campaign issues.

Rather than imposing ideas of 'progress' and 'development' on individuals and communities throughout the world, people themselves should be able to choose the way they want to live without being made to feel that they are somehow 'inferior' or 'backward' by not following a pattern that has been adopted elsewhere (Willis, 2005: 112).

True grassroots development with access to the right form of social and economic capital could break the mould of programmatic funding and restrictive criteria. It would give people more ownership of their community, and thus increase their power.

Conclusion

In this chapter we have acknowledged the strengthening position of community development within an Irish policy context and highlighted some of the challenges faced in bringing about real and lasting social change. At times, these challenges seem insurmountable. The challenge to us as workers is daunting but no more daunting than the dread of not knowing where you will sleep tonight or where the next dinner is coming from. We must continue to connect with the lived reality of people experiencing exclusion and isolation and ensure that those with decision-making authority are exposed to this reality. Unless the work is meaningful to them and they can see and feel the effects of poverty and exclusion on individuals there is a danger that they will remain aloof and distant from the impact of their decisions. Thus a critical issue is organisational culture and the place of corporate ethos and values in bodies that are part of the social inclusion delivery system. At all levels there should be an understanding and appreciation of community development and what it is trying to achieve.

The strengthened position of community development gives an opportunity for those most excluded to be at the decision-making table. Supporting target group participation in decision-making processes should continue to be a key aim of community development, which in turn will create interface opportunities and develop bridging social capital. This has the potential to break stereotypes and challenge the subtle distinctions that lead to exclusionary behaviour. However, we need to be aware of the limitations that can arise from the Petri dish model and start to create greater networking opportunities that can amplify community power. This can only be achieved by bringing other significant social actors into the domain of social inclusion work.

Stimulating organic change and facilitating the expansion of social, cultural and economic capital is a difficult task that will require dedicated individuals who have the courage to challenge the status quo and believe in the strength of real communities, not just non-governmental organisations or Partnerships. Ideally, if authentic change is achieved at the local level—and by that we mean a shift in power—this could then influence regional and national change. We have seen from the work of the former homeless leaders in Chicago that such change is possible. The work of the Eldonian Community Trust highlights the need to find new ways of investing in our communities, ways that will enable them to generate and direct income, to reduce their dependence on government funding and develop the skills and capacities to develop and grow their community for future generations. If this entails the transfer of assets from statutory bodies, then the lessons need to be learnt from what is happening in the UK.

There is currently considerable interest in the transfer of land and building assets from statutory and other public agencies to independent, community-based, not-for-profit organisations. This is focused on the contribution asset transfer can make to a wide range of social and economic policy objectives—at national, regional and local level (Hart, 2001: 2).

Trying new approaches to community development must take into account the uniqueness of each community and the wider social context. Nevertheless, we cannot afford to dismiss any approach with a cursory glance or a dismissive remark. This itself belittles the work of other practitioners attempting to tackle similar issues in other countries. We must continue to develop our capacity and enlarge our toolbox to ensure we have the knowledge, resources and ideas to take on the task. If this means looking outside or abroad, then this needs to be done. Ultimately, our hope is to contribute to a conversation about the need to promote the values and ethos of community development, facilitate greater opportunities for interaction between social groups, identify more sustainable funding mechanisms and, finally, support grassroots movements.

There is no doubt that the challenges facing community development in Ireland are significant, as indeed are the challenges facing those trying to bring about social change. Sometimes activists and practitioners can find themselves ostracised or isolated for the path they have taken. Indeed, resistance or conflict is at times an indicator of progress, albeit a difficult one to manage. Yet despite the challenges, community development is garnering broader support as a means to bring about social inclusion. There are significant supports available for community development approaches including the Community Development Programme and the Local Development Social Inclusion Programme. As practitioners, we must acknowledge this and work with communities to use the available resources wisely. As Saul Alinsky stated: 'Tactics means doing what you can with what you have' (Alinsky, 1971: 126).

Conclusions

CHAPTER 11

State and civil society in Ireland: conclusions and mapping alternatives

Peadar Kirby and Mary Murphy

The end of Ireland's economic boom provides an opportunity critically to assess the nature of the state–civil society relationship as it has evolved, and to offer perspectives on how it might change in the immediate future. This is the purpose of this chapter. We begin by summarising what the book has told us about the nature of the relationship between state and civil society in Ireland as we put the Celtic Tiger period behind us. We then illustrate some examples of the consequences of the type of state–civil society relationship that became dominant in Ireland over the past two decades, identifying some worrying absences. The following section theorises the symbiotic relationship between state and civil society and how they have mutually constituted themselves with outcomes that are ever more evident throughout Irish society. The chapter finishes by mapping some alternative ways in which the relationship could be transformed that would be more beneficial for civil society and for the wider Irish society.

The state–civil society relationship today

Four conclusions emerge from this book about how the state and civil society have interacted over the past two decades. They are contributed by various authors but are consistent across the range of contributors to the book, thus reinforcing their weight. Each is treated in turn, drawing on previous chapters by way of illustration.

(1) A controlling relationship

In Chapter 3, Brian Harvey traces the evolution of the state–civil society relationship over the decades, drawing attention to the 'many

evolutions, changes of course, u-turns, inconsistencies and adjustments' that have characterised it. He refers to the promise of the first
formal policy document on the role of civil society which finally appeared in 2000, endorsing the right of civil society organisations to
independence and freedom of action, and to the ability to speak out
on issues that concern them. However, soon afterwards it became
evident that policy was moving in the opposite direction, as a services
paradigm began to dominate the role that the state envisaged for civil
society. As Harvey puts it: 'Increasingly, the relationship between the
state and civil society came to be defined around services' while, at the
same time, organisations that received state funding—including those
concerned with overseas development, Travellers, and childcare—
were told to cease criticising government if they wanted to continue
to receive funding. Harvey offers evidence of an ever more restrictive
and controlling regime being imposed on charitable organisations
summed up in the sinister phrase 'non-adversarial partnerships' used
by the National Economic and Social Council in 2005. As he puts it,
'that the Irish state fears a civil society that might dare try, in its words,
to "persuade" speaks volumes of its multiple insecurities.'

In Chapter 4, Mary Murphy comments that the Irish state has retained and even increased its power over civil society and is 'restructuring local civil society in its own interests' rendering community
work and local development work 'vulnerable to the manipulations
of the state'. She concludes that the Irish state's strategy 'to co-opt,
control, dis-empower and attempt to effectively cognitively lock Irish
civil society has been largely successful'. Martin Geoghegan and Fred
Powell in Chapter 8 place this strategy in the context of 'the hegemonic discourse of social partnership' over the past two decades to
which alternative approaches such as local development initiatives and
civil society community action had to accommodate themselves. They
therefore present the Irish state's approach as just one approach and see
local development initiatives and community action as alternatives.

(2) Ever more disciplinary funding regimes

It is in the terrain of funding that this state control is most clearly exercised. Murphy identifies a politicisation of the funding regime for
community and voluntary sector organisations and a discernible shift
in funding to organisations that provide services. Furthermore, Harvey
shows how the state's desire to control the community and voluntary

sector was first demonstrated in funding cutbacks and in unilateral changes to well-established funding arrangements, and he comments that the sector was 'taken aback by the manner and vindictiveness' of these actions. The growth in state funding for the community and voluntary sector over the past two decades and the ever greater dependence of the sector on such funding comes therefore at great cost to the sector and to the quality of Irish democracy. Also, it is becoming more and more evident that the state is using funding to impose its agenda in a very disciplinary way, a practice that makes a mockery of the ubiquitous discourse of 'partnership'. Little partnership has been evident in the state's decisions on funding for the sector over recent years.

(3) State wants service provision model

For various contributors to this book, the thrust of the Irish state's policy towards civil society is to move it from concerns with redistributive justice and social change towards the provision of services, usually in some kind of partnership with the state.

Geoghegan and Powell describe the process as the 'reinvention of community development as consumerist welfare provision rather than developmental active citizenship'. They conclude that the managerialist logic of social service provision orients active citizenship away from political activism and points it towards 'more socially conservative conceptions of active citizenship that emphasise "self-reliance"', thereby reasserting the pre-eminence of the state in the social partnership policy paradigm.

For the practitioners of community development, this situation raises particular challenges. Catherine Murray and Paul Rogers write in Chapter 10 that funding is increasingly for service interventions and not for capacity building. They add that this approach to funding is 'myopic in that it drip feeds funding into communities and ensures a dependency culture when we should be looking towards independence and long-term sustainability'. Furthermore, they say they are 'faced with the realisation that despite a significant commitment to social inclusion, there is little evidence that this commitment has become part of the dominant culture and ethos of many statutory bodies and other organisations working from a social inclusion remit', something which finds expression in the 'restrictive criteria of key programmes'.

In his examination of a far wider set of social movements in Chapter 7, Mark Garavan interestingly identifies a fundamental range of issues to which the Irish state is deaf, that it does not want to hear from civil society. Examining controversies over incinerators, for example at Poolbeg in Dublin, electricity pylons such as those proposed for Meath, and the Corrib gas pipeline in Mayo, he writes: 'It seems that lots of community actors seem to be very annoyed about lots of specific issues and are well capable of expressing their disgruntlement.' Yet, while these actors appear to have very little difficulty in articulating their position, Garavan argues that instead of being able to generate a deep debate on fundamental issues such as the meaning of development, the value of community or the purpose and implications of our economic models, 'they are instead forced onto far narrower discursive ground'. This he illustrates through examining the discourse between the various stakeholders in the Corrib gas dispute in north Mayo since 2000, concluding that in this conflict between community actors on the one side and the state and large multinational corporations on the other, 'it becomes clear that critical issues animating the conflict are often not heard at all'.

The state's evident desire to restrict civil society actions to service provision is therefore doing a great disservice to Irish society as it drives into oppositional channels the rich contribution that civil society has to make to the fundamental questions facing the society, questions of justice, equality and models of development. Again, this contradicts the rhetoric of partnership and shows a state that is unable to be self-critical and to engage in learning. It is a most ominous portent for the future as, due to the economic downturn, the state is losing its ability to stifle dissent through throwing money at it. May it seek more repressive ways of doing this?

(4) Blinkered and obfuscating ideology

In Chapter 6, Michael Cronin examines the meanings that lie behind the use of the concept of 'active citizenship' by the Irish state. Examining the deliberations of the Taskforce on Active Citizenship, he finds that what the term hides is any understanding of the unequal distribution of power in Irish society so that what is presented is a highly individualised and idealised picture of the power of individuals. Murphy makes a similar point when she writes of the failure of the state's discourse on social capital to address power inequalities between communities. As Cronin puts it: 'Such individualisation of problems has the dual advantage of concealing the real power differentials between different players in society ("you have just as much responsibility as a Tony O'Reilly") and making politics a continuation of market forces where what matters most is consumer preference and the sustainability of Brand Ireland.' As a result, what the Taskforce presents are 'sets of symptoms with no identifiable causes' so that, by refusing to provide a critical context for the understanding of the operations of the market economy, it deals with problems it can neither understand nor resolve. 'The result is that the active citizen is left to believe in a familiar credo of Faith (in the current politico-economic setup) and Good Works (volunteering).' This illustrates well the blinkered and obfuscating nature of the benign rhetoric with which the Irish state has cloaked itself over the era of the Celtic Tiger—appearing to be friendly to citizens and their needs but neglecting entirely the situation of growing inequality in power and resources created by its policies, and actively discouraging any questioning of this situation by its citizens.

Geoghegan and Powell elaborate on the implications of this ideology for the provision of services. Examining the treatment in the Taskforce report of three key issues—equality, political engagement, and governance—they identify a communitarian and neo-liberal view equating citizenship 'with a voluntaristic, depoliticised notion of civil society based upon promoting social capital'. They add that the 'relationship between the state and civil society in terms of governance is underpinned by a neo-liberal managerialist view of social service provision'. They identify the key state concern that drives this ideological configuration as follows:

> What is emerging is a form of welfare where the ideology of neo-liberal and communitarian civil society, of *community*, eclipses the idea of a politically active civil society, binding social actors together in the name of the national project of 'partnership' i.e. of making Ireland attractive for international investment (emphasis in original).

This identifies the Irish state's real priorities and the reason why it limits the activities which it wants to allow civil society to engage in.

In Chapter 5, John Baker maps out a more challenging agenda for Irish society, focusing on the issue of equality. He maintains that 'the kinds of equality that have become central to Irish discourse and legislation are primarily the weakest forms of liberal egalitarianism—such as anti-discrimination legislation and means-tested support for basic needs—as distinct from stronger forms of liberal egalitarianism and radical ideals of equality of condition.' From another angle, this again shows the limits of the Irish state's view and, by making such limits transparent, helps to show just how restricted it is. As he writes: 'Like many other political concepts, there are more and less challenging conceptions of equality, and it is generally the less challenging forms that have become familiar. However, the fact that equality is back on the political agenda provides an opportunity to press for more ambitious goals.' This clearly opens up grounds for a more contestatory form of active citizenship promoting much more ambitious goals and putting pressure on the state to achieve them.

Consequences and absences

Some civil society organisations actively seek a new regulatory relationship with the state. Others struggle to maintain a wider and more political understanding of their role but are thwarted by the very regulatory framework that they seek to resist. There have been many practical manifestations of the loss of dynamism in civil society over recent years. The following discussion outlines a number of key 'absences' in the Irish state/society dynamic that, when combined, illustrate the scale of the task facing Irish civil society organisations that wish to reconstitute their relationship with the state.

(a) Absence of political dynamic

Shively (2007: 64) argues that civil society is the natural counterweight to government in the affairs of the state and often the space from which spontaneous movements develop to oppose government policies. A review of the experience of the civil society movements in both Eastern Europe and Latin America illustrates that it is not unrealistic to see such movements give birth to new political movements. However, so far this has not happened in Ireland. There is recent evidence of some civil society groups seeking to develop more overtly political strategies across environmental, service charge, regeneration and anti-development issues in local authority areas. This grassroots 'ground up' organising through umbrella groups like People before Profit represents a new space and a new strategy for Irish civil society and has already given rise to some new political dialogue. Whether it can be sustained over a long period, and go on to develop broader political coalitions with anti-poverty and equality sectors and other political actors, remains to be seen.

(b) Absence of national reform campaigns

It was argued earlier that the present relationship between state and society can be understood as the outcome of a long historical trajectory where civil society mirrored a state that is predominately populist in culture and clientelistic in forms of acting. Hardiman (1998: 122) argues that if we want to understand the relative lack of progress in redressing inequalities we need a 'closer analysis of the patterns of interest representation in the form of party policies and interest group formation'. Taking as an example that part of civil society concerned with social welfare issues, it is instructive to observe how it has organised itself not as a unified political force but rather mirrors the state's social welfare categories—farmers, unemployed, lone parents, and those with a disability. Like the contingent nature of the social security system, the agenda of each civil society group tends to be one-dimensional. While some larger national organisations maintain a coherent institutional engagement with the state, most social welfare activity is focused on state-controlled processes, chief among them the annual pre- and post-budget 'listening' forums where up to 40 diverse and often small groups make budget submissions. It is commonly acknowledged that discourse in this process is 'voice without influence' (Lister, 2004) that 'has not proved enough to change policy priorities' (Hardiman, 1998: 142). This sub-sector of civil society, because its organic development has mirrored the state's own structures, does not have the power of a well-organised vested interest to influence policy. Similar observations can be made about the fragmented nature of lobbies in the health, disability, education and housing sectors.[1] This general absence of a national umbrella group dedicated to cross-sectoral campaigning on specific social policy issues is noticeable when compared to civil society practices in other countries.

(c) Absence of civil society as a positive voice in the Lisbon Referendum campaign

The experience of the 2008 Lisbon referendum campaign is instructive about the health of civil society and shows how a potentially

---

1 In the British context, both Whiteley and Winyard (1987) and Levitas (1988) observed the ease with which governments consciously play groups off against each other and the importance of members of the British anti-poverty sector acting as a single unified lobby.

beneficial and interdependent relationship between state and society can be diluted to become weak and dependent. At least some of the discourse in the Lisbon referendum points to the presence of an active and independent civil society that was strong enough to provide an effective counter discourse to the established and mainstream body politic. There is also evidence, as suggested by new social movement theory, of a relatively healthy participatory democracy with the ecological and anti-military movements offering new and alternative ways of organising.

However, on closer inspection, it appears that the only civil society groups with active campaigning positions in the Lisbon Referendum were those which were against the Treaty. These were groups independent of the state and without a structured relationship with it in terms of funding or service-delivery contracts. Conversely, civil society organisations dependent on state funding appeared not to want, or felt unable, to participate directly in this key campaign. While some groups like European Anti-Poverty Network (EAPN) Ireland[2] and CORI led strong information campaigns, generally civil society groups in structured policy or funding relationships with the state stayed silent on Lisbon. This implies that some civil society organisations feel implicit or explicit restrictions on their freedom to take political positions in national debates. It reflects a tradition in Irish civil society where groups are careful not to align themselves to political parties, a tradition that McCashin et al (2002) relate back to the tendency of the populist Fianna Fáil to co-opt civil society.

Contributors to this volume have argued that a legacy of Fianna Fáil's hold on power over the last two decades has been an intensification of this historical tendency to depoliticise civil society. Since 2002 the state has become more ambitious in this regard. This strong direc-

---

2 The Irish European Anti-Poverty Network, with the support of the Communicating Europe Initiative of the Department of Foreign Affairs, organised three regional meetings in Tallaght, Sligo and Tipperary, and a national roundtable on the social dimension of the Lisbon Treaty in May 2008. It published an EAPN Ireland 'Review' with articles from a broad range of contributors from all sides of the debate on various dimensions of the Treaty from a social perspective, placing it in the context of developing a social Europe. It also made a 22-page submission to the National Forum on Europe which highlighted the debate on the social implications of the Lisbon Treaty. CORI, a significant voice in Irish social debate, also published a briefing paper in which they stated that 'we never recommend how people should cast their vote but we strongly believe that people should vote'.

tive control of the state has arguably had the greatest impact on that part of civil society most traditionally associated with the community and voluntary sector. Ironically, these very groups may have had most positive exposure to the benefits of Europe (they directly benefited from EU funding, they have been exposed to EU institutions and, through their membership of European networks, they express solidarity with other marginalised groups in the Union). Has the state depoliticised and silenced the very voices it might most like to hear from in a second referendum? It is healthier for democracy if civil society is contributing to debate from many perspectives and not only from the more extreme spectrums on both the left and the right.

(d) The absence of conflict in social partnership

Over the Celtic Tiger period, social partnership processes have monopolised the context in which distributional debate has happened. Some credit social partnership as being the cause of Ireland's more humane welfare trajectory, relative to the UK or the US. Others argue that social partnership can, through co-option, limit protest and smother the potential for more radical change. The period generally has been described as a missed opportunity when the state, despite enjoying the greatest resources ever available, generally pursued a relatively inegalitarian fiscal policy. This highlights just how little influence social actors in many forums of social partnership have really had on key state policy. Rather, social partnership was used to establish and maintain an elite-driven consensus that failed to achieve a fair balance between goals of efficiency and equity in the Irish political economy.

This consensus was and is achieved through institutional processes designed to produce and maintain consensus at the expense of processes that might generate conflict about distributional policy. It is done by maintaining a strong narrative of shared understanding where 'social partners leave ideological differences outside the door and problem solve in the context of a shared understanding'(NESF 1997). In this way the state, explicitly and implicitly, by controlling funding and filtering social partnership participation, mitigates dissent from such hegemonic shared understanding. Participation in social partnership offers special challenges to civil society organisations which understandably wish to maximise opportunities for 'voice with influence' but also wish to avoid the smothering embrace of the state (Broaderick, 2002).

(e) Absence of political debate

Anne Marie Smith (1998: 7) argues that 'political struggle does nevertheless depend in part on the ability to imagine alternative worlds'. It is
not just through social partnership that the Irish state minimises political debate. The state, by way of funding strategies, has helped to create a
monopoly role for some institutions in Irish discourse. Economic and
Social Research Institute (ESRI) analysis, for example, underpins social
partnership (NESF and NESC) and anti-poverty institutions (Office
for Social Inclusion). Kirby (2002) argues that ESRI analysis of poverty
and social inclusion is epistemologically rooted in classical economics
theory. The dominant poverty debate concerns technical issues about
work incentives and replacement ratios, definitions and measurement
of unemployment, definitions and measurement of poverty/inequality
and, most recently, labour market impacts of migration. This narrow
policy discourse limits public debate and acts as a barrier to entry into
the policy community. It is possible to identify an alternative discourse
about rights, equality and social spending and a discourse promoting
family values, parenting and responsibility but this is far less promi-
nent. Again, historical trajectories are important in understanding the
present. The Catholic social teaching which focused, in the early years
of the state, on more absolutist forms of poverty reduction and charity
(Acheson et al., 2004) is directly correlated with modern political
acceptance of 'solidarity without equality' (Ó Riain and O'Connell,
2000:39). The impact of a shift to more individual values associated
with neo-liberalism has further eroded societal support for equality.

The 2008 attempt to silence one of the most independent au-
thoritative voices on poverty, that of the Combat Poverty Agency,
is illustrative of how the state responds to any form of dissent from
consensus on how to frame discourse on poverty. Combat Poverty
has been a distinctive voice in Irish discourse promoting a wider and
more humane discourse about poverty. From 2002 the state removed
various functions from the Agency including its community development remit and and its role in funding anti-poverty networks. The
state increasingly sought to control its public statements, requiring all
press statements to be screened for veto by the Minister for Social and
Family Affairs. Finally in 2008, the Office for Social Inclusion established a seven-person review committee which, without due process
and without considering alternative options, proposeed to subsume
the Combat Poverty Agency into the Department of Social and

Family Affairs. This attempt was made when the poor were at their most vulnerable. Such a 'reform' of the Agency would make it part of a government department and would directly lead to a significant loss of its ability independently to identify and analyse the causes of poverty, comment independently and authoritatively on it, objectively monitor and evaluate progress in tackling it and promote public awareness of it. It would also undermine the working relationship with community and voluntary sector groups working to tackle poverty. It therefore calls into question the principle of consultation with the poor which, according to the state's rhetoric, lies at the heart of the Irish partnership approaches to anti-poverty policy. Since other alternatives were available to government (such as transferring the Combat Poverty Agency to the National Economic and Social Development Office), it seems that the state is using the opportunity of reform of its agencies to weaken the equality, rights and anti-poverty agencies that have played a powerful watchdog role for the most poor and vulnerable in our society.

State and civil society: a symbiotic relationship

The contributors to this book have thrown light on how state–civil society relationships have evolved over the period of the Celtic Tiger. What emerges is a picture of a state ever more determined to use its power to constitute a role for civil society that makes it subservient to the state, providing services to some of the most needy in Irish society (often on completely inadequate budgets and lacking any long-term security) but never daring to raise a critical voice about the glaring and scandalous injustices of that society, injustices it knows only too well from its daily activities. In doing this, the state's priority is to make Ireland safe for investment by multinational companies and to stifle any debate about the social impacts of the highly dependent model of development promoted by the Irish state.

In elaborating this critique, this book can be said to adopt a civil society view of the state. Clearly, a book that drew on the views of state authorities towards civil society would offer very different perspectives and it would be a very valuable exercise to undertake. Yet, whichever perspective is adopted, it is important to continuously bear in mind that the state has the whip hand in this relationship due to its control of funding (and, of course, its far greater ideological and coercive power). Clearly, as all the contributors have highlighted in different ways, the state exercises a lot of influence over the ways that civil society constitutes and organises itself, the goals it pursues and the means through which it pursues them. For example, in Chapter 3 Brian Harvey reminds us of a much more empowering and contestatory form of civil society activity that emerged from the Irish state's sponsoring of the National Pilot Projects to Combat Poverty in the late 1970s, a programme that the state then killed off in the early 1980s when it became too uncomfortable to deal with. This reminds us of the power of the state in constituting civil society and the inadequacy of any view that sees civil society as a discrete entity that firstly constitutes itself and then afterwards establishes relationships with the state. Any reflection on the nature of Irish civil society, therefore, whether in the pre-independence period covered by Ó Broin and Kirby in Chapter 2, the period following independence as briefly surveyed by Harvey, or the Celtic Tiger period which is the principal focus of this book, must take into account the ways in which the state helped constitute civil society. For example, it was the British colonial state that opened the spaces and even provided some of the organisational and funding possibilities that allowed a vibrant and creative civil society to flourish over the final decades of the 19th century and into the first decades of the 20th. It is paradoxical in the extreme that a civil society activism that played such a key role in the emergence of an independent Irish state, should then be stifled and become highly dependent on that state for most of the 20th century.

Making this point reminds us that the state–civil society relationship is not a one-way street. It is not only that the state helps constitute civil society but also that civil society helps constitute the sort of state that exists. Ó Broin and Kirby illustrate how this happened in the immediate pre-independence period but the same point can be made about the sort of Irish state that emerged and remained dominant up to the period of the early Celtic Tiger. Particularly following the arrival of Fianna Fáil to electoral dominance in 1932, the Irish state came to be characterised by its finely honed ability to co-opt potentially dissident elements (and where this was not possible to make life so difficult for them that they often emigrated) through piecemeal and often small-scale projects and spending. This may have ensured that a conservative civil society faced few challenges but it also meant that the state notoriously lacked the capacity for longer term planning, reacting to problems as they emerged rather than developing the ability for proactive planning. Particularly since the economic liberalisation of the early 1960s, the state has been remarkably dependent on outside economic interests, again illustrating the weak development of the capacities of civil society and also the lack of sustained pressure from civil society to constitute a more activist state. As is widely recognised, the independent Irish state became populist in its culture and clientelist in its predominant forms of acting.

Clearly, civil society is not the only influence on constituting the state (outside influences such as multinational corporations or the EU, the legacies of history, and the nature of its own bureaucracy and political system also play major roles) but it is a major influence and it is difficult to explain the sort of state that emerged in Ireland in the 20th century without appreciating this point (see Adshead, Kirby and Millar, 2008). For example, a more independent and critical civil society would have challenged the dominance of Irish politics by Fianna Fáil and Fine Gael and would have pressurised the Irish state to develop a more coherent and integrated welfare state. Acknowledging that not only does the state help constitute civil society but also that civil society in turn helps constitute and change the state draws attention to the importance of civil society resisting the subservient relationship and role into which it is currently being pushed. For, without a more activist and challenging civil society, it is difficult to know what influences could help constitute a state capable and willing of addressing with some determination the huge challenges of equality and sustainability it has so shamefully neglected.

An analysis of contributions in this volume enables us to theorise further the state/civil society relationship at the end of the Celtic Tiger and draw tentative conclusions about the health or otherwise of that relationship. We have argued that, relative to the social transformation role played by civil society at the foundation of the state, the relationship has been less political and mutually reciprocal and is more one-sided and dependent. It is also increasingly market-oriented. The value of civil society to the state has become one dimensional. The state's interest in nurturing civil society is limited to a very narrow understanding of active, citizenship, namely volunteering and providing social services.

Quo vadis?

Geoghegan and Powell (2007: 48) argue that there is potential for a renewed discourse about alternatives and for active citizenship to re-imagine itself as a democratic force. This section examines how this might be progressed. Is it possible to recreate the vibrant role civil society organisations played in the emergence of the Irish state (see Chapter 2)? What can be done to ensure that political and policy alternatives emerge from civil society? Acheson et al. (2004: 197) argue that to date the Irish state has played a key role 'in structuring the civic space in which voluntary action occurs'. When the institutional space in which civil society does its work is largely state controlled, meaningful distributional debate is limited (Acheson et al., 2004). This raises the question of where and how civil society organisations position themselves in relation to the state. At least two things appear obvious. Firstly, civil society needs resources that are independent of the state. Secondly, civil society needs to organise itself in free space that is designed for and by itself.

Taking the first question first, how to break free of state control, the challenge is to break the historical trajectory described in these chapters and to struggle free from the cultural and ideological forces that have shaped Irish voluntary action and its development. Three strategies are required: organisation-level funding, individual-level political activity, and giving greater voice to the reality of poverty and inequality.

(a) Civil society organisations need to enhance their ability to resist the implicit and explicit threats to funding that do indeed occur when groups vocalise counter-hegemonic discourse. Harvey's paper in this volume and the contemporary debate about the Charities Act illustrates the real and serious problems facing organisations seeking alternative funding sources to those of the state. Recognising that such strategies can be 'frightening and unpredictable', Ledwith (2005: 7) encourages groups to feel the fear and take up the challenge. The challenge here is to identify what conditions will enable civil society actors and groups to take the level of risk required to break free of state-controlled spaces and discourses. The question of solidarity is important as is Daly's advice to work cross-sectorally, building links between largely separate spheres of civil society, for example, trade unions, new social movements, political parties and community and voluntary groups (Daly, 2007). This requires actively listening to each other and denying the state space proactively to build divisions between different groups within civil society.

(b) The above comment is primarily about organisational decisions. However, civil society organisations are managed by people, staff and volunteers, who are also citizens. As members of civil society each has their own individual relationship with the state, each votes, each can join a political party or take part in a protest march. If the challenge for civil society actors is to revive the very concept of active citizenship that the state is trying to bury, then there are personal as well as organisational challenges in doing this. The Irish state thrives on an apolitical civil society where many key actors go out of their way to demonstrate to the state their political neutrality. Taking up the challenge of radical participative democratic values means being open as staff, volunteers, residents and citizens to being politically active in civil society, with or without state funding. Despite the funding and institutional obstacles described earlier much can be done, not only as professional workers but also through voluntary political activity.

(c) Irish political culture promotes a non-ideological approach to political debate where political decisions about redistribution are reduced to technical statistical debates and where the dominant macro discourse revolves around competitiveness and employment growth. This discourse happens largely in exclusive spaces away from the public ear. A change in strategy is required to move debate outside closed policy forums or social partnership processes and into more public realms. These public realms could include more extensive use of media (such as newspaper letter writing campaigns or radio talk shows), and of local and national public meetings. The focus of such communication should be not be technical debates but telling it like it is, voicing the reality of what it means to be poor or unequal in Ireland today and promoting the values that matter to civil society groups. This would result in a value-led communicative discourse.

The second question focused on how civil society can organise itself in some free space that is designed for and by civil society: how might it choose to restructure?

Again three possible strategies emerge: rethinking social partnership strategies, organising in large cross-sectoral interest groups, and developing new political movements.

(a) If the present institutional shape of civil society, dominated as it is by social partnership, militates against articulating an effective political discourse, then what can be done about this? Within civil society groups there are always tensions about strategy and whether to develop integrationist or conflict approaches to relationships with the state. A key debate in Irish civil society is whether or not to participate in social partnership. One way of approaching this is to avoid all or nothing choices of whether one should or should not participate. Rather, mindful of the tendency of social partnership to smother or silence political discourse, the question might be better rephrased as when and for what purposes should one participate in partnership processes? Here we can distinguish the policy or problem-solving function of partnership from a more political function of partnership as a forum for redistributive political debate. Following Larragy (2001), redistributive political decisions in particular are better kept for the publicly accountable representative political system. This line of reasoning suggests civil society groups need to use social partnership sparingly and in particular to avoid inappropriate use of the social partnership processes to develop policy that is more appropriately developed through public political dialogue and, when necessary, political conflict .

(b) Given the sensitivity of the Irish Proportional Representation electoral system to well-organised sectoral interests, the challenge for civil society groups is how they can organise into more proactive long-term interest groups. For example, a national campaign for welfare reform could be built through a permanent coalition of the 40 or so groups which have a recognised interest in social security reform. This could move from a strategy of ineffective short-term pre-budget submissions towards more individual, personal engagement between lobbyists and civil servants (Acheson et al., 2004: 101). The sector was most influential when working through larger advocacy coalitions. The opposite is also true; when conflicting approaches were recognisable within the sector, governments manipulated the palpable differences as an excuse for doing nothing. Joint policy development work across organisations would maximise the sector's power as a vested interest capable of influencing electoral outcomes.

(c) What of civil society's role in spawning political opposition and being the traditional birthplace of new political movements? Is there capacity in Ireland for civil society to develop a new left-oriented political movement or movements? There are emerging political spaces in Irish civil society. These include new social movements, new self-organised identity-based movements including new migrants' movements and, as explored earlier, new alliances of previously unconnected groups such as People before Profit. Some of these groups have formed alliances with academic and trade union communities. The Irish social science academic community has formed an Irish Social

Science Platform, a by-product of which may be an enhanced contribution to public debate (see Kirby, 2008). Existing groups like the Community Platform continue to develop strategies to work together. TASC, a think tank for action of social change, has made public its interest in making alliances and promoting political debate. The Labour Party has established a Commission for the 21st century, examining its relationships with civil society actors like trade unions and is open to transforming and renewing itself as a political movement. A number of NGOs working on international issues—Comhlámh, the Debt and Development Coalition Ireland, the Africa Centre and the Latin America Support Centre (LASC)—have founded a new global justice movement, Bloom. The spontaneous marches and meetings against health and education cuts in autumn 2008 shows the potential from protests that still exists. All of these different dynamics are to date unplanned and ad hoc and there is no clear direction emerging. However, one fact can be stated with certainty: there is a critical mass of people interested in and actively working for urgent social change. Blyth (2002) and Hay (2004) argue that moments of transformation occur when critical junctures or opportunities arise and when people are organised sufficiently to affect political debate and promote ideas that make sense in the context of that critical juncture. In the autumn of 2008, we saw emerging such a critical juncture in the global and national political economy. The opportunity is ripe for a new left-wing social movement to rise to the challenge of being a natural counterweight to a political status quo that has generated such inequality, risk and vulnerability in people's lives .

Civil society organisations work best as the autonomous space between the market and the state. They influence the nature of political economy models and help ensure a better trade-off between efficiency and equity considerations. While civil society actors often play a powerful role in organising a counter-discourse and influencing a state's political dynamic, they are also an important partner for states in attempting to manage in an increasingly complex globalised world. The problem in Ireland is that the historical trajectory of a deeply controlling state has muted civil society's capacity to be socially transformative. While this may have some short-term political advantage for the state, it has long-term disadvantages for all.

Bibliography

Acheson, Alan (2002): *A History of the Church of Ireland 1691–2001*, Dublin: Columba Press.

Acheson, Nicholas, Brian Harvey, James Kearney and Arthur William-son (2004): *Two Paths, One Purpose: Voluntary Action in Ireland, North and South*, Dublin: Institute of Public Administration.

Acheson, Nicholas, Brian Harvey and Arthur Williamson (2005): 'State welfare and the development of voluntary action: the case of Ireland North and South', in *Voluntas: International Journal of Voluntary and Non Profit Organisations*, Vol. 16, No. 2, pp. 181–202.

Adshead, Maura, Peadar Kirby and Michelle Millar (2008): 'Ireland as a model of success: contesting the Irish state', in Maura Adshead, Peadar Kirby and Michelle Millar (eds) *Contesting the State: Lessons from the Irish case*, Manchester: Manchester University Press, pp 1–24.

Ahern, Bertie, 2006, Speech by An Taoiseach, Bertie Ahern TD, announcing the membership of the Taskforce on Active Citizenship, 18 April 2006., last accessed 5 January 2009.

Alinsky, Saul (1971): *Rules for Radicals*, Random House, New York.

Allen, Kieran (2000): *The Celtic Tiger: The Myth of Social Partnership in Ireland*, Manchester: Manchester University Press.

Allen, Kieran (2007): *The Corporate Takeover of Ireland*, Dublin: Irish Academic Press.

Anderson, Benedict (1991): *Imagined Communities*, London: Verso.

Area Development Management (2000): *Local Development Social Inclusion Programme Guidelines 2000–2006*, Dublin: ADM.

Baccaro, Lucio and Marco Simoni (2004): *The Irish Social Partnership and the 'Celtic Tiger' Phenomenon*, Geneva: International Institute for Labour Studies.

Baker, John, Kathleen Lynch, Sara Cantillon and Judy Walsh (2004): *Equality: From Theory to Action*, Basingstoke: Palgrave Macmillan.

Barber, Benjamin (1984): *Strong Democracy: Participatory Politics for a New Age*, University of California Press, California.

Barnard, Toby (2004): *The Kingdom of Ireland 1641–1760*, Basingstoke: Palgrave Macmillan.

Benhabib, Seyla (2002): *The Claims of Culture: Equality and Diversity in a Global Era*, Princeton, NJ: Princeton University Press.

Blyth, Mark (2002): *Great Transformation: Economic Ideas and Institutional Change in the Twentieth Century*, Cambridge: Cambridge University Press.

Bon, Veronica (2006): *The Endorsement Process*, Limerick: Mid West Community Development Support Agency.

Boyce, D. G. (1996): *The Irish Question and British Politics 1868–1996*, Basingstoke: Palgrave Macmillan.

Broaderick, Sheelagh (2002): 'Community development in Ireland: a policy review', in *Community Development Journal*, Vol. 37, No. 1, pp. 101–110.

Buck, Nick, Ian Gordon, Alan Harding and Ivan Turok (2005): *Changing Cities: Rethinking Urban Competitiveness, Cohesion and Governance*, Basingstoke: Palgrave Macmillan.

Callanan, Mark and Justin F. Keogan (2003): *Local Government in Ireland Inside Out*,

Dublin, Institute of Public Administration.

Cantillon, Sarah, Carmel Corrigan, Peadar Kirby and Joan O'Flynn (2001): *Rich and Poor: Perspectives on Tackling Inequality in Ireland, Dublin*: Combat Poverty Agency/Oak Tree Press.

Central Statistics Office, 2007: *Quarterly National Household Survey Quarter 3 2006: Module on Sports and Physical Exercise*, Dublin: CSO.

Cerny, Philip G. (2002): *Globalization at the Micro Level: The Uneven Pluralization of World Politics,* Manchester Papers in Politics: CIP Series 5/2002.

Chambers, Edward (2003): *Roots for Radicals: Organizing for Power, Action and Justice*, New York: Continuum.

Clark, Terry (2003): 'Globalisation and transformations in political cultures', in Robin Hambleton, Hank Savitch and Murray Stewart (eds): *Globalism and Local Democracy*, Basingstoke: Palgrave Macmillan, pp. 67–94.

Clarke, Susan (2003): 'Globalism and cities: a North American perspective', in Robin Hambleton, Hank Savitch, and Murray Stewart (eds): *Globalism and Local Democracy*, Basingstoke: Palgrave Macmillan, pp. 30–51.

Coleman, Shane (2006) 'Is our democracy being hoodwinked?', *Sunday Tribune*, 17 September, p. 16.

Collins, Tom (1993): 'The community sector and partnership with the state' in Seán Healy and Brigid Reynolds (eds) *New Frontiers for Full Citizenship* Dublin: Conference of Major Religious Superiors, pp. 86–105.

Combat Poverty Agency (2000): *The Role of Community Development in Tackling Poverty,* Dublin: Combat Poverty Agency.

Community Workers Co-operative (2001): *Local Social Partnership Analysis*, Galway: Community Workers Cooperative.

Community Workers Co-operative (2005): *CWC Draft Annual Report 2005,* Galway: Community Workers Cooperative,
last accessed: 25 June 2008.

Compston, Hugh (2002): 'The strange persistence of policy concertation' in Stefan Berger and Hugh Compston (eds.) *Policy Concertation and Social Partnership in Western Europe,* Oxford and New York: Berghan Books.

Connolly, Eithne (2007): *The Institutionalisation of Anti-Poverty Policy in the Social Partnership Process*, Dublin: Combat Poverty Agency.

Conroy, Pauline (1994): *Progress Through Partnership*, Dublin: Combat Poverty Agency.

Cosgrove, Sharon and Niamh Ryder (2001): *Community and voluntary sector involvement in the new local authority structures: survey report for the Local Government Anti-poverty Learning Network,* Dublin: Combat Poverty Agency.

Cronin, Michael (2004): 'Babel Átha Cliath: the languages of Dublin', in *New Hibernia Review*, Vol. 8, No. 4, winter 2004, pp. 9–22.

Crowley, Niall (1996): 'Frameworks for Partnership' in P. Conroy et al., *Partnership in Action*, Galway: Community Workers Co-operative.

Crowley, Niall (1998): 'Partnership 2000: empowerment or co-option?' in Peadar Kirby and David Jacobson (eds) *In the Shadow of the Tiger*, Dublin: Dublin City University Press, pp. 69–82.

Currie, Glynis (2008): 'Concerned for Programme's future', in *Changing Ireland*, Issue 26, summer 2008, pp. 22–23.

Daly, Mary and Nicola Yeates (2003): 'Common origins, different paths: adaptation and change in social security in Britain and Ireland', in *Policy and Politics,* Vol. 31,

No. 1, pp. 85–87.

Daly, Siobhán (2007): 'Mapping civil society in the Republic of Ireland', in *Community Development Journal*, Vol. 43, No. 2, pp. 157–176.

Dani, Anis A. and Arjan De Hann (2008): *Inclusive States: Social Policy and Structural Inequalities* (New Frontiers of Social Policy Series), Washington: World Bank Publications.

De Zengotita, Thomas (2005): *Mediated: How the Media Shape Your World*, London: Bloomsbury.

Delanty, Gerard (2000): *Citizenship in a Global Age: Society, Culture, Politics*, Buckingham: Open University Press.

Dillow, Chris (2007): *The End of Politics: New Labour and the Folly of Managerialism*, Petersfield: Harrriman House.

Doherty, Joe, Pascal de Decker, Volker Busch-Geertsema, Eoin O'Sullivan, Ingrid Sahlin, Antonio Tosi, Sakari Hänninen and Sirkka-Lisa Kärkkäinen (2005): *The Changing Role of the State—Welfare Delivery in the Neo-liberal Era,* Brussels: FEANTSA.

Donoghue, Freda (1999): *Uncovering the Non-profit Sector in Ireland: Its Economic Value and Significance*, Baltimore: John Hopkins University Press.

Drier, Peter (2007): 'Community empowerment strategies: the limits and potential of organising in low income neighbourhoods', in Elizabeth Strom and John Mollenkopf (eds) *The Urban Politics Reader,* London: Routledge, pp. 191–203.

Dukelow, Fiona (2002): 'From social exclusion to social inclusion? Tracing the historical development of social citizenship in the North and South of Ireland', in *Administration*, Vol. 50, No. 2, pp. 41–66.

Edmondson, Ricca (2007): 'Rhetorics of social science: sociality in writing and inquiry', in Stephen Turner and William Outhwaite (eds) *Sage Handbook of Social Science Methodology,* London: Sage, pp. 959–1007.

Edmondson, Ricca (2008): 'Intercultural rhetoric, environmental reasoning and wise argument' in Ricca Edmondson and Henrike Rau (eds) *Environmental Argument and Cultural Difference: Locations, Fractures and Deliberations*, Bern: Peter Lang AG, pp. 337–394.

Eldonians, The (2007): last accessed 27 April 2007.

Elliott, Anthony and Charles Lemert (2006): *The New Individualism: The Emotional Costs of Globalization*, London: Routledge.

Environmental Protection Agency. 2007. *CO2 EPA Emission Factors.* EPA: Wexford. http://www.epa.ie/downloads/pubs/air/airemissions/name,12097,en.html, last accessed 5 January 2009.

Fahey, Tony (2007): 'How do we feel? Economic boom and happiness', in Tony Fahey, Helen Russell and Christopher T. Whelan (eds) *The Best of Times? The Social Impact of the Celtic Tiger*, Dublin: Institute of Public Administration, pp. 11–26.

Farrell, Clare (2007): 'Thinking critically about social capital', in *Irish Journal of Sociology,* Vol. 16, No. 2, pp. 27–49.

FitzGerald, Garret (2008): 'It is in our interests to teach immigrants English', in *The Irish Times*, 9 February 2008.

FitzGerald, John (2000): 'The story of Ireland's failure—and belated success' in Brian Nolan, Philip J. O'Connell and Christopher T. Whelan (eds.) *Bust to Boom? The Irish Experience of Growth and Inequality*, Dublin: Institute of Public Administration.

Fitzgerald, Mary (2007): 'Research identifies language as key barrier to fuller integration', in *The Irish Times*, 23 August 2007.

Fitzpatrick Associates (2006): *Final Review of the RAPID Programme*, Dublin: Department of Community, Rural and Gaeltacht Affairs.

Forde, Catherine (1996): 'History of community work', in Paul Burgess (ed.) *Youth and Community Work: A Course Reader,* Cork: UCC Centre for Adult and Continuing Education, pp. 3–13.

Forde, Catherine (2005): 'Local democracy or local administration? Irish local government reform 1996–2004' in Peter Herrmann and Frank Columbus (eds.) *Applied Social Studies: Recent Developments, International and Comparative Perspectives,* New York: NOVA Science.

Foucault, Michel (2001): *Madness and Civilisation.* London: Routledge Classics.

Gallagher, Seán (2000): 'P. J. Meghan and approved local councils: a neglected experiment in community development', in *Administration,* Vol. 48, No. 2, 77–91.

Garavan, Mark (ed.) (2006a): *The Rossport Five: Our Story*, Dublin: Small World Media.

Garavan, Mark (2006b): 'Seeking a real argument', in Mary P. Corcoran and Michel Peillon (eds): *Uncertain Ireland: A Sociological Chronicle, 2003–2004*, Dublin: Institute of Public Administration, pp. 73–90.

Garavan, Mark (2007): 'Resisting the costs of "development": local environmental activism in Ireland', in *Environmental Politics*, Vol. 16, No. 5, November 2006, pp. 844–863.

Garavan, Mark (2008): 'Problems in achieving dialogue: cultural misunderstandings in the Corrib gas dispute', in Ricca Edmondson and Henrike Rau (eds) *Environmental Argument and Cultural Difference: Locations, Fractures and Deliberations*, Bern: Peter Lang AG, pp. 65–92.

Geoghegan, Martin and Fred Powell (2007): 'Active citizenship, civil society and the enabling state: political myth or democratic reality', in *Administration*, Vol. 55, No. 3, pp. 31–51.

Gittell, Ross and Avis Vidal (1998): *Community Organizing: Building Social Capital as a Development Strategy*, Newbury Park, California: Sage Publications.

Government of Ireland (1996): *Better Local Government, A Programme for Change,* Dublin: Department of the Environment and Local Government.

Government of Ireland (1997): *Sharing in Progress: National Anti-Poverty Strategy*, Dublin: The Stationery Office.

Government of Ireland (1997): *Supporting Voluntary Activity: A Green Paper on the Community and Voluntary Sector and its Relationship with the State*, Dublin: The Stationery Office.

Government of Ireland (2000): *Supporting Voluntary Activity: A White Paper on a Framework for Supporting Voluntary Activity and for Developing the Relationship between the State and the Community and Voluntary Sector,* Dublin: Government Stationery Office.

Government of Ireland (2003): Department of Community, Rural and Gaeltacht Affairs, Press Release
, last accessed 25.06.2008

Government of Ireland (2007): *National Development Plan 2007–2013*, Dublin: NDP/ CSF Information Office.

Government of Ireland (2007): *Taskforce on Active Citizenship Report to Government*, Dublin: Government Stationery Office.

Grant, Wyn (1989): *Pressure Groups, Politics and Democracy in Britain*, Hemel Hemsptead: Philip Allan.

Grootaert, Christiaan (1998): *Social Capital: The Missing Link?* Social Capital Initiative Working Paper No. 3, Washington DC: World Bank.

Hambleton, Robin (2003): 'The New City Management', in Robin Hambleton, Hank Savitch and Murray Stewart (eds) *Globalism and Local Democracy*, Basingstoke: Palgrave Macmillan, pp. 147–168.

Hambleton, Robin, Hank Savitch and Murray Stewart (eds) (2003): *Globalism and Local Democracy*, Basingstoke: Palgrave Macmillan.

Hardiman, Niamh (1998): 'Inequality and representation of interests', in William Crotty and David Schmitt (eds) *Ireland and the Politics of Change*, London: Longman, pp. 122–155.

Hardiman, Niamh (2001): 'Social Partnership, wage bargaining and growth' in Brian Nolan, Philip O'Connell and Christopher T. Whelan (eds) *Bust to Boom: The Irish Experience of Growth and Inequality*, Dublin: Institute of Public Administration, pp. 286–309.

Hart, Lorraine (2001): *Asset Transfer: A Can-Do Guide,* Development Trust Association
, last accessed 27 June 2008.

Harvey, Brian (2002): *The Role of the Community Sector in Local Social Partnership*, Dublin: ADM.

Harvey, Brian (2003): *Report on Implementation of the White Paper 'Supporting Voluntary Activity'*, Dublin: CV12.

Harvey, Brian (2007): 'Community development: a tool for anti-poverty work', in *Community Development: A Tool for Anti-Poverty Work in Ireland*, Tralee: South and Mid West Community Development Support Agency, pp. 8–13.

Harvey, Brian (2008): 'Community sector funding', paper accessed directly from the author; available from Peadar Kirby (peadar.kirby@ul.ie).

Hastings, Tim, Brian Sheehan and Padraig Yeates (2007): *Saving the Future: How Social Partnership Shaped Ireland's Economic Success*, Dublin: Blackhall Publishing.

Hay, Colin (1999): 'Crisis and the structural transformation of the state: interrogating the process of change' in *British Journal of Political Science and International Relations,* Vol. 1, No. 3, pp. 317–344.

Hay, Colin (2004): 'Ideas, interests and institutions in the comparative economy of great transformations', in *Review of International Political Economy,* Vol. 2, No. 1, pp. 204–206.

Hayward, Katy (2006): 'The politics of adaptation in Ireland' in Katy Hayward and Muiris MacCarthaigh (eds) *Recycling the State: The Politics of Adaptation in Ireland*, Dublin: Irish Academic Press, pp. 1–17.

Healy, Alison (2007): 'Most people still using car to get to work', *The Irish Times*, 29 June 2007.

Healy, Kieran (1998): 'The new institutionalism: Irish Social Partnership', in Seán Healy and Brigid Reynolds (eds) *Social Policy in Ireland: Principles, Practice and Problems*, Dublin: Oak Tree Press, pp. 59–84.

Held, David, Anthony McGrew, David Goldbatt and Jonathan Perraton (1999): *Globalisation, Politics, Economics and Culture*, Cambridge: Polity.

Hill, Jacqueline (1980): 'The Protestant response to Repeal: the case of the Dublin working class' in T. W. Moody and R. A . J. Hawkins (eds) *Ireland under the Union: Varieties of Tension: Essays in Honour of T. W. Moody*, Oxford: Oxford

University Press, pp. 35–68.

Hoffmann-Martinot, Vincent and Jefferey Sellers (eds)(2005): *Metropolitanization and Political Change*, Wiesbaden: Verlag für Sozialwissenschaften.

Hogan, T. (2005): 'Diplomat raises stink over sewage station', in *Fingal Independent* 30 August 2005:
, last accessed 10 June 2008.

Holmes, Finlay (2000): *The Presbyterian Church in Ireland*, Dublin: Columba Press.

Home Office Development and Statistics Directorate (2004): *2003 Home Office Citizenship Survey: People, Families and Communities*, Home Office Research Study 289. Available online at
accessed 5 June 2008.

Honohan, Iseult (2005): 'Active citizenship in contemporary democracy', in Clodagh Harris (ed.) *The Report of the Democracy Commission: Engaging Citizens, The Case for Democratic Renewal in Ireland*, Dublin: TASC/New Island, pp. 169–180.

Hoppen, Theodore (1989): *Ireland since 1800: Conflict and Conformity*, Harlow: Longman.

House, John D. and Kyla McGrath (2004): 'Innovative governance and development in the new Ireland: social partnership and the integrated approach', in *Governance* 17 (1), pp. 29–57.

Hughes, Gerard, Frances McGinnity, Philip O'Connell and Emma Quinn (2007): 'The impact of migration', in Tony Fahey, Helen Russell and Christopher T. Whelan (eds) *The Best of Times? The Social Impact of the Celtic Tiger*, Dublin: Institute of Public Administration, pp. 217–244.

Hulme, David and Michael Edwards (1997): *NGOs, States and Donors: Too Close for Comfort?* London: Macmillan.

Ingold, Timothy (2000): *The Perception of the Environment: Essays on Livelihood, Dwelling and Skill*, London: Routledge.

Jackson, Alvin (1999): *Ireland 1798–1998*, Oxford: Blackwell.

Jacobsen, John Kurt (1994): *Chasing Progress in the Republic of Ireland: Ideology, Democracy and Dependent Development,* Cambridge: Cambridge University Press.

Jensen, Per H. and Birgit Pfau-Effinger (2005): '"Active" citizenship: the new face of welfare' in Jorgen Goul Anderson, Anne-Marie Guillemard, Per H. Jensen and Birgit Pfau-Effinger (eds) *The Changing Face of Welfare,* The Policy Press: Bristol.

Jessop, Bob (1999): 'The changing governance of welfare: recent trends in its primary function, scale and methods of coordination', *Social Policy and Administration*, Vol. 33, No. 4, pp. 348–359.

Jessop, Bob (2002): *The Future of the Capitalist State*, Oxford: Blackwell Publishing.

Jones, Chris and Tony Novak (1999): *Poverty, Welfare and the Disciplinary State,* Routledge: London.

Joyce, James (1977): *Ulysses*, London: Penguin.

Kelly, Philip (2001): 'The Irish Social Partnership system', paper presented at Public Service Association of New Zealand conference 'Partnership in the Modern Public Service' in Wellington, New Zealand, June 2001,   ,
last accessed 1 November 2007.

Kennelly, Brendan and Eamon O'Shea (1997): 'Efficiency, values and social welfare policy' *Administration*, Vol. 45, No. 2, pp. 3–20.

Keogan, Justin (2003): 'Reform in Irish Local Government' in Mark Callanan and Justin Keogan (eds): *Local Government in Ireland: Inside Out*, Dublin: Institute of Public Administration.

Keohane, Kieran and Carmen Kühling (2004) *Collision Culture: Transformations in Everyday Life in Ireland*, Dublin: Liffey Press.

Kirby, Peadar (2001): 'Inequality and poverty in Ireland: clarifying social objectives' in Sarah Cantillon, Carmel Corrigan, Peadar Kirby and Joan O'Flynn (eds) *Rich and Poor: Perspectives on Tackling Inequality in Ireland*, Dublin: Oak Tree Press.

Kirby, Peadar (2002): *The Celtic Tiger in Distress: Growth with Inequality in Ireland*, Basingstoke: Palgrave.

Kirby, Peadar (2005): 'Globalisation, vulnerability and the role of the state: lessons for Ireland', in *Administration,* Vol. 52, No. 4, pp. 49–68.

Kirby, Peadar (2008a): Seminar presentation at University College Cork, February 2008; available from Peadar Kirby (peadar.kirby@ul.ie).

Kirby, Peadar (2008b): 'Raising the larger questions: challenges for the social sciences in post-Celtic Tiger Ireland', keynote address to the first annual conference of the Irish Social Sciences Platform, Dublin City University, 11 September 2008; available from Peadar Kirby (peadar.kirby@ul.ie).

Kirby, Peadar, Luke Gibbons and Michael Cronin (2002): 'The reinvention of Ireland: a critical perspective' in Peadar Kirby, Luke Gibbons and Michael Cronin (eds) *Reinventing Ireland: Culture, Society and the Global Economy*, London: Pluto Press.

Kirby, Peadar and Mary Murphy (2008): 'Ireland as a competition state' in Maura Adshead, Peadar Kirby and Michelle Millar, (2008) *Contesting the Irish State*, Manchester University Press, pp. 120–142.

Kolb, Eberhard (1988): *The Weimar Republic*, London: Routledge.

Landry, Charles and Geoff Mulgan (1994): *Themes and Issues: The Future of the Charities and Voluntary Sector*, Working Paper 1, Deinos, London.

Larragy, Joe (2001): 'Civil society versus market in Irish social policy', paper presented to Irish Social Policy Association annual conference, Trinity College Dublin, 27 July 2001, available at   last accessed 5 January 2009.

Larragy, Joe (2006): 'Origins and significance of the community–voluntary pillar in Irish Social Partnership' in *The Economic and Social Review*. Vol. 37, No. 3, pp. 375–398.

Laval, Christian (2007): *L'Homme économique: essai sur les racines du néolibéralisme*, Paris: Gallimard.

Ledwith, Margaret (2005): *Community Development: A Critical Approach*, Bristol: Policy Press.

Lee, Anna (2006): *Community Development: Current Issues and Challenges*, Dublin: Combat Poverty Agency,
                                     , last accessed 17 June 2008.

Lepine, Eileen, Ian Smith, Helen Sullivan and Marilyn Taylor (2007): 'Neighbourhoods and governance' in Ian Smith, Eileen Lepine and Marilyn Taylor (eds) *Disadvantaged by Where You Live? Neighbourhood Governance in Contemporary Urban Policy* Bristol: Policy Press.

Levitas, Ruth (1998): *The Inclusive Society; Social Inclusion and New Labour*, Basingstoke, Palgrave.

Lister, Ruth (2004): *Poverty,* Cambridge: Polity Press.

Luddy, Mary (1995): *Women and Philanthropy in Nineteenth Century Ireland*, Cambridge: Cambridge University Press.

Mac Cormaic, Ruadhán (2008): 'Study of multi-ethnic school identifies language barrier as biggest challenge', in *The Irish Times* 18 February 2008.

Macionis, John and Ken J. Plummer (1997): *Sociology: A Global Introduction,* New Jersey: Prentice Hall Inc.

Mandell, Betty Reid (2002): *The Privatization of Everything*, New Politics ix (1) pp. 83–100.

Marcuse, Herbert (1964): *One-Dimensional Man*, London: Routledge and Keegan Paul.

Mathews, P. J. (2003): *Revival: The Abbey Theatre, Sinn Féin, The Gaelic League and the Co-operative Movement*, Cork: Cork University Press.

Maume, Patrick (1999): *The Long Gestation: Irish Nationalist Life 1891–1918*, Dublin: Gill & Macmillan.

McAleese, Mary (2007): 'Remarks by President McAleese to open the Immigrant Council of Ireland Discussion on Migration "The Richness of Change: Gaining from Migration in 21st Century Ireland"'. Available online: accessed 6 May 2008.

McCashin, Anthony, E. O'Sullivan and C. Brennan (2002): 'The NESF social partnership and policy formation in the Republic of Ireland', in *Policy and Politics*, Vol. 30, No. 2, pp. 264–277.

McCashin, Anthony (2004): *Social Security in Ireland*, Dublin: Gill & Macmillan.

McCready, Sam (2000): *Empowering People: Community Development and Conflict, 1969–1999,* Coleraine: University of Ulster Centre for Voluntary Action Studies; Dublin: The Stationery Office.

McDonald, Frank (2007): 'Report shows up grim reality of Ireland's greenhouse gas record', in *The Irish Times*, 16 February 2007.

McLoughlin, Thomas (2005): *Contesting Ireland: Irish Voices against England in the Eighteenth Century*, Dublin: Four Courts Press.

Meade, Rosie (2005): 'We hate it here, please let us stay! Irish Social Partnership and the community voluntary sector's conflicted experiences of recognition', in *Critical Social Policy* 25 (3), pp. 349-73.

Montague, Pat (2001) 'Persuasive influence: an assessment of how Irish groups campaign around the budget', unpublished master's thesis, Dublin City University.

Moran, Marie, (2005): 'Social exclusion and the limits of pragmatic liberalism', discussion paper to conference on 'Equality, Care and Social Inclusion', University College Dublin/Queens University Belfast, 24 June 2005; amended version available from Irish Political Studies.

Morrissey, Thomas (2002): Book review of *Vocationalism and Social Catholicism in Twentieth-Century Ireland: The Search for a Christian Social Order,* in *Catholic Historical Review*, 88 (1), 150–153.

Moulaert, Frank (2000): *Globalization and Integrated Area Development in European Cities*, Oxford: Oxford University Press.

Mulhall, Daniel (1999): *A New Day Dawning: A Portrait of Ireland in 1900*, Cork: The Collins Press.

Murphy, Mary (2002a): 'Social partnership: is it the only game in town?', in *Community Development Journal* Vol. 37, No 1, pp. 80–91.

Murphy, Mary (2002b): 'Community involvement in the Social Partnership process', presented at the annual conference of the Irish Social Policy Association, Dublin on 5 December 2002, available from Deiric Ó Broin (deiric.obroin@dcu.ie).

Murphy, Mary (2007): 'The challenge of institutional change in urban governance: supporting social innovation', paper delivered to Political Studies Association of Ireland/*Journal of Irish Urban Studies* conference 'Urban Politics in Ireland:

Reflections on Theory and Practice' on 6 June 2007 in Dublin City University, available from Deiric Ó Broin (deiric.obroin@dcu.ie).

Murphy, Mary and Peadar Kirby (2008): 'A better Ireland is possible: The challenge of voicing an alternative vision for Ireland', available from Peadar Kirby (peadar.kirby@ul.ie).

Murphy, Mary and Michelle Millar (2007): 'The NESC developmental welfare state: opportunity or threat?', in *Administration*, Vol. 55, No 3, pp. 75–100.

Murphy, Mary and Deiric Ó Broin (2008): 'Square pegs and round holes: Dublin City's experience of the RAPID programme', paper delivered at the workshop, Metropolitan Governance and Social Inequality, ECPR Rennes 11–16 April 2008; available from Deiric Ó Broin (deiric.obroin@dcu.ie).

Murray, Frank and Paddy Teahon (1997): 'The Irish political and policy-making system and the current programme of change' in *Administration*, Vol. 45, No. 4, pp. 39–58.

Murray, Michael (2006): 'The polluter pays? Individualising Ireland's waste problem', in Mary P. Corcoran and Michel Peillon (eds.) *Uncertain Ireland: A Sociological Chronicle, 2003–2004*, Dublin: Institute for Public Administration.

Natali, David and Martin Rhodes (1998): *New Politics of the Bismarckian Welfare State-Pension Reform in Continental Europe*, EUI: Florence.

National Economic and Social Council (1999): *Opportunities, Challenges and Capacities for Choice,* Dublin: NESC.

National Economic and Social Council (2005a): *The Developmental Welfare State*, Report No. 113, Dublin: NESC.

National Economic and Social Council (2005b): *People, Productivity and Purpose*, Dublin: NESC.

National Economic and Social Forum (1997): Report No 16 *A Framework for Partnership: Enriching Strategic Consensus through Participation*, Dublin: Government Publications Office.

National Economic and Social Forum (2003): Report No. 28, *The Policy Implications of Social Capital*, Dublin: Government Publications Office.

National Economic and Social Forum (2006): Report No. 33 *Creating a More Inclusive Labour Market*, Dublin: Government Publications Office.

Newman, Janet (2000): 'Beyond the new public management' in John Clarke, Sharon Gewirtz and Eugene McLaughlin, *New Managerialism: New Welfare?* Sage: London.

Nolan, Brian, Philip O'Connell and Christopher T. Whelan (eds) (2000): *Bust to Boom. The Irish Experience of Growth and Inequality*, Institute of Public Administration, Dublin.

Obama, Barack (2006): *The Audacity of Hope*, New York: Three Rivers Press.

Ó Broin, Deiric and Eugene Waters (2007): *Governing Below the Centre: Local Governance in Ireland*, Dublin: TASC/New Island.

O'Carroll, J. P. (2002): 'Culture lag and democratic deficit in Ireland, Or dats outside the terms of the agreement', in *Community Development Journal* Vol.37, No.1, pp 10–19.

Ó Cinnéide, Seamus (1998): 'Democracy and the Constitution', in *Administration* 46 (4), 41–58.

O'Connor, Orla and Mary Murphy (2008): 'Women and social welfare' in Ursula Barry (ed.), *Where Are We Now: Feminist Debate in Contemporary Ireland*, Dublin: TASC/New Island.

O'Connor, Pat (2000): 'The Irish patriarchal state: continuity and change', in Maura Adshead, Peadar Kirby and Michelle Millar (eds) *Contesting the State: Lessons from the Irish Case*, Manchester, Manchester University Press, pp. 143–164.

O'Donnell, Rory (2000): 'The new Ireland in the new Europe', in Rory O'Donnell, (ed.): *Europe: The Irish Experience*, Dublin: Institute of European Affairs, pp. 161–214.

O'Donnell, Rory (2006): 'Social Partnership in Ireland' presented at NewGov 'Policy learning and Experimentation' conference in London, England, 26 March 2006, available at www.eu-newgov.org/Econpol/ECONPOL_PractForum_0306_ Presentations/ NEWGOV_Pract-Forum_0306_Pres03_ODonnell.pps last accessed 5 January 2009.

O'Donnell, Rory (2008): 'The partnership state: building the ship at sea', in Maura Adshead, Peadar Kirby and Michelle Millar (eds), *Contesting the State: Lessons from the Irish Case*, Manchester, Manchester University Press, pp. 73–99.

O'Ferrall, Fergus (2000): *Citizenship and Public Service: Voluntary and Statutory Relationships in Irish Healthcare*, Dublin: The Adelaide Hospital Society; Dundalk: Dundalgean Press.

Offe, Claus (1984): *Contradictions of the Welfare State*, Hutchinson, London.

O'Hearn, Denis (1998): *Inside the Celtic Tiger: The Irish Economy and the Asian Model*, London: Pluto.

O'Hearn, Denis (2001): *The Atlantic Economy: Britain, the US and Ireland*, Manchester: Manchester University Press.

Ohmae, Kenichi (1995): *The End of the Nation-State*, New York: Free Press.

O'Leary, Don (2000): *Vocationalism and Social Catholicism in Twentieth Century Ireland*, Dublin: Irish Academic Press.

Open University (2008) *Cultural Capital and Social Exclusion.*
last accessed 25 June 2007.

O'Regan, Michael (2005): 'Harvard professor my guru since early 1990s, says Ahern', in *The Irish Times*, 3 September 2005.

Organisation for Economic Co-operation and Development (2001): *The Well Being of Nations: The Role of Human and Social Capital,* Paris: OECD.

Organisation for Economic Co-operation and Development (2008): *Ireland: Towards an Integrated Public Service,* Paris: OECD.

Ó Riain, Seán and Philip O'Connell (2000): 'The role of the state in growth and welfare', in Brian Nolan et al. (eds) *Bust to Boom: The Irish Experience of Growth and Inequality*, Dublin, Institute of Public Administration, pp. 310–339.

O'Sullivan, Michael (2006): *Ireland and the Global Question*, Cork: Cork University Press.

Ó Tuathaigh, Gearóid (1990): *Ireland before the Famine 1798–1848*, Dublin: Gill & Macmillan.

Paseta, Senia (1999): *Before the Revolution: Nationalism, Social Change and Ireland's Catholic Elite 1879–1922*, Cork: Cork University Press.

Peace, Adrian (1993): 'Environmental protest, bureaucratic closure: the politics of discourse in rural Ireland', in K. Milton (ed.) *Environmentalism: The View from Anthropology*, London and New York: Routledge, pp. 189–204.

Peillon, Michel (2001): *Welfare in Ireland: Actors, Resources and Strategies*, Connecticut and London: Praeger.

Pierre, Jon (2000): *Debating Governance: Authority, Steering and Democracy*, Oxford:

Oxford University Press.

Pierson, Paul (1994): *Dismantling the Welfare State: Reagan, Thatcher and the Politics of Retrenchment,* Cambridge: Cambridge University Press.

Pierson, Paul (1996): 'The new politics of the welfare state', in *World Politics* Vol. 48, No. 2, pp. 143, 179.

Pierson, Paul (1998): 'Irresistible forces, immovable objects: post industrial welfare states confront permanent austerity', in *Journal of European Social Policy* Vol. 5, No. 4, pp. 539–60.

Pierson, Paul (1999): *Post Industrial Pressures on the Mature Welfare States*, WS/44, Florence: European University Institute.

Pierson, Paul (2001): *The New Politics of the Welfare* State, Oxford: Oxford University Press.

Polanyi, Karl (2001): *The Great Transformation: The Political and Economic Origins of our Time*, Boston: Beacon Press (original 1944).

Popple, Keith (1995): *Analysing Community Work: Its Theory and Practice*, Milton Keynes: Open University Press.

Powell, Fred and Martin Geoghegan (2004): *The Politics of Community Development*, Dublin: A. & A. Farmar.

Putnam, Robert (2000): *Bowling Alone: The Collapse and Revival of American Community*, New York: Simon and Schuster.

Rawls, John (1999): *A Theory of Justice* (revised edition), Oxford: Oxford University Press.

Redmond, Declan, Veronica Crossa, Niamh Moore and Brendan Williams (2007) *Dublin as an emergent global gateway: Pathways to creative and knowledge-based regions* ACRE report, Amsterdam: AMIDSt, University of Amsterdam.

Roche, William and Terry Cradden (2003): 'Neo-corporatism and social partnership', in Maura Adshead and Michelle Millar (eds): *Public Administration and Public Policy in Ireland: Theory and Methods,* London: Routledge, pp. 64–81.

Roseneil, Sasha and Fiona Williams (2004): 'Introduction to special issue', in *Social Politics*, Vol. 11, No. 2, pp. 147–153.

Roy, Arundhati (2003): *War Talk*, Boston: South End Press.

Ruddle, Helen and Freda Donoghue (1995): *The Organisation of Volunteering*, Dublin: NCIR Press.

Sabel, Charles (1996): *Local Partnerships and Social Innovation*, Paris: OECD.

Sabel, Charles (1998): 'Foreword', in Peadar Kirby and David Jacobson (eds): *In the Shadow of the Tiger*, Dublin: Dublin City University Press, pp xi–xiii.

Sassen, Saskia (1991): *The Global City,* Oxford: Oxford University Press

Sassen, Saskia (2001): *The Global City: New York, London, Tokyo*, Princeton: Princeton University Press.

Sassen, Saskia (2004): *Cities in a World Economy*, London: Sage.

Sassen, Saskia (2007): 'Economic restructuring as class and spatial polarisation', in Elizabeth Strom and John Mollenkopf (eds) *The Urban Politics Reader*, San Francisco: Routledge, pp. 28–41.

Scholte, Jan Aart (2005): *Globalization; A Critical Introduction*, Basingstoke: Palgrave Macmillan.

Sen, Amartya (1999): *Development as Freedom*, Oxford: Oxford: University Press.

Sennett, Richard (1998): *The Corrosion of Character: The Personal Consequences of Work in the New Capitalism*, New York: Norton.

Shively, W. Phillips (2007): *Power and Choice: An Introduction to Political Science*, New

York: McGraw Hill.

Skidmore, Paul and John Craig (2005) 'Start with people: How community organizations put citizens in the driving seat', London: Demos.
accessed 5 January 2009.

Smith, Anne-Marie (1998): *Laclau and Mouffe: The Radical Democratic Imaginary*,
London: Routledge.

Smith, Nicola Jo-Anne (2005) *Showcasing Globalisation? The Political Economy of the
Irish Republic*, Manchester: Manchester University Press.

Stewart, A. T. Q. (2001): *The Shape of Irish History*, Belfast: Blackstaff Press.

Sugrue, Karen (2006): 'Why prison fails', in Mary P. Corcoran and Michel Peillon
(eds.) *Uncertain Ireland: A Sociological Chronicle, 2003–2004*, Dublin: Institute for
Public Administration, pp. 43–57.

Swank, Duane (2002): *Global Capital, Political Institutions and Policy Change in
Developed Welfare States*, Cambridge: Cambridge University Press.

Sweeney, Paul (2008*): Ireland's Economic Success: Reasons and Lessons*, Dublin: New
Island Press.

Tansey, Paul (1998): *Ireland at Work: Economic Growth and the Labour Market
1987–1997*, Dublin: Oak Tree Press.

Taskforce on Active Citizenship (2006), *Background Working Paper*, Dublin: Taskforce
on Active Citizenship.

Taskforce on Active Citizenship (2007): *Report to Government*, Dublin: Taskforce on
Active Citizenship.

Taylor, George (2002): 'Negotiated governance and the Irish polity', in George Taylor
(ed.) *Issues in Irish Public Policy*, Dublin: Irish Academic Press, pp. 28–51.

Taylor, George (2005): *Negotiated Governance and Public Policy in Ireland,* Manchester:
Manchester University Press.

Tovey, Hilary (2001): 'The co-operative movement in Ireland: reconstructing civil
society', in Hilary Tovey and Michel Blanc (eds) *Food, Nature and Society: Rural
Life in Late Modernity*, Aldershot: Ashgate, pp. 321–338.

Ward, Alan (1994): *The Irish Constitutional Tradition*, Dublin: Irish Academic Press.

Whelan, Irene (2005): *The Bible War in Ireland: The Second Reformation and the
Polarization of Protestant-Catholic Relations 1800–1840*, Dublin: Lilliput Press.

Whiteley, Paul and Stephen Winyard (1987): *Pressure for the Poor: The Poverty Lobby
and Policy Making,* London: Methuen.

Wilden, Anthony (1980): *The Imaginary Canadian*, Vancouver: The Pulp Press.

Wilkinson, Richard G. (1996) *Unhealthy Societies: The Afflictions of Inequality*,
London: Routledge.

Willis, Katie (2005): *Theories and Practices of Development*, New York: Routledge.

Yeates, Nicola (2002): *Globalisation and Social Policy,* London. Sage.

Young, Iris Marion (2000) *Inclusion and Democracy*. Oxford: Oxford University Press.

INDEX

social action, 26, 97
social teaching, 116–17, 152
Celtic Tiger, 24, 63, 68, 143, 147
ethos, 113–14
and neo-liberal values, 38
and social partnership, 102, 151, 153–5
and state-civil society relationships

Central Applications Office (CAO), 55
Centre for Effective Services, 30
Centre for Public Inquiry, 32
Cerny, 40
Charitable Bequest Act, 1844, 15
charities, 31
Charities Act, 156
Cherish, 27
Chicago, 135–6, 137, 138
child care, 31, 54, 57, 144
Christian Brothers, 16
Church of Ireland
    disestablished, 14–15, 16, 23
    power of, 11–13
Churchill, Winston, 112
citizenship. see also active citizenship
    reactive, 74–5
    status, 53
Citizenship Referendum, 2004, 73, 75, 76
civic republicanism, 5, 62, 63–4, 101, 110
civil service, 119, 121–2, 158
civil society
    contemporary, 3–6
    contested meaning of, 95–110
    definitions, 35
    development of, 4, 9–24
        1870–1923, 16–21
        19th c., 9–16
    dissent in Ireland, 25–33
    impact of globalisation, 34–47
    increased activism needed, 124–5
    independent funding needed, 156–7
    lack of political dynamic, 148
    lack of reform campaigns, 149
    and Lisbon Referendum, 149–51
    orientation, 100–1
    and political argument, 78–91
    restructuring, 157–9
    service provision model, 145–6
    and social partnership, 24

and the state, 3–6, 21, 23, 29–32, 143–8, 153–5
    conclusions, 143–59
    strategies, 157–8
civil war, 21
Claidheamh Soluis, An, 20
Clark, Terry, 42
clientelism, 65–6, 149, 155
climate change, 66, 70, 71
Clondalkin Partnership, 74
co-operatives, 18, 20, 23, 25, 96
cohesion process, 106–9, 128
Coillte, 88
Combat Poverty Agency (CPA), 126, 152–3
Comhlámh, 159
Commission on Active Citizenship, 104
Commission on Social Welfare, 26, 29
Commission on Vocational Organisation, 116–17
Commissioners of Public Instruction, 14, 15
commodification, 45, 67
Communicating Europe Initiative, 150n
Communism, 32, 51
communitarianism, 4–5, 62, 63–4, 107, 110, 147
Community, Rural and Gaeltacht Affairs, Department of, 28, 40–1, 43, 98, 106, 120n
community action, 5, 133–4
    and social partnership, 121
    strategy, 97–8
    20th c. Ireland, 25–7
Community Action Network, 120
Community-Based Drugs Initiatives, 98–9
Community Councils, 96
community development, 3, 4, 6, 27–8, 132–3
    current status, 127–8
    definitions, 35
    economic capital, 136–7
    funding, 144–5
    and liberal egalitarianism, 51–61
    local democratic renewal, 103–5
    and meaning of civil society, 95–110
    networking, 133–4
    objectives of, 60

INDEX

INDEX

social class, 75–6
social exclusion, 2–3, 22, 26
 Petri dish model, 129–30
 reasons for, 130–2
social inclusion, 40, 98, 128–9, 145
social partnership, 5, 6, 27, 95, 144, 145
 absence of conflict, 151
 acceptance of, 114–17
 assessment of, 102–3
 civil society orientation, 100–1
 community development strategy, 97,
  98–100
 contested understandings of, 111–14
 critiques of, 117–24
 effects of, 24, 46
 emergence of, 98–100
 functions of, 158
 institutionalisation, 5–6, 111–25
 power in, 105, 119–22
 state orientation, 101–2
 voluntary sector in, 28–9, 36–8
social policy, 25–6
Social Security (White Paper), 26, 29
Social Service Councils, 96
Social Welfare, Department of, 26
Society of St Vincent de Paul, 16
sports, 9, 69
SSIA scheme, 121n
state
 control by, 34, 143–4, 150–1
  community development, 95, 109–10
  funding threats, 44, 47, 127–8, 144–5,
   151
  how to escape, 156–7
  local governance, 41–3
  social partnership, 36–8, 101–2, 103,
   122–3
  voluntary sector, 39–41
 ideology of, 146–8
 relationship with civil society, 143–59
 response to dissent, 152–3
Statoil, 85
Strategic Management Initiative (SMI),
 102
Strategic Policy Committees (SPCs), 101,
 102, 104–5
Strategy for Recovery (NESC), 118
street protest, 5–6, 111, 125, 159

subsidiarity, 116n
Sugrue, Karen, 65
Supporting Voluntary Activity (White
 Paper), 28, 40, 101–2, 108
Sustaining Progress, 118
Swank, Duane, 36
Swift, Jonathan, 11

Tallaght, Dublin, 30, 150n
TASC, 159
Taskforce on Active Citizenship, 4–5,
 63–4, 101–2, 146–7
 global contexts, 68–71
 and immigration, 72, 73–4, 75
 reports, 64–8, 106–8
taxation, 122
Taylor, George, 112, 115
Terenure College, 16
territorial nationalism, 69
Thatcher, Margaret, 36, 51, 100
time, attitudes to, 86–90
Tipperary, County, 150n
tithes, 14–15
Today Tonight, 118n
Tovey, Hilary, 18, 20
trade mark, 18
trade unions, 99, 113, 156, 158
 and Labour Party, 159
 and the state, 36–7
Travellers, 31, 53, 57, 144
Treaty debate, 21
tribunals of enquiry, 54
Trinity College Dublin (TCD), 19
Trócaire, 31n
Tuam, County Galway, 15

unemployment, 24, 27, 62, 99, 114, 149
 outsourcing, 36
Unionism, 13
United Irishmen, 62
United Kingdom (UK), 28, 32, 37, 100,
 112, 115, 126, 151, 154
 anti-egalitarianism, 51
 anti-poverty sector, 46, 149n
 community development, 136–7, 139
 Home Office, 64
 New Labour, 123
 social partnership, 97

[181]